Eleventh Hour Chronicles

Ruby Lee Sanders

Ruby Lee Sanders

Copyright © 2019 Ruby Lee Sanders
All rights reserved.
ISBN: 978-0-578-48269-9

Illustrator: Janasia House; janaisiahouse@gmail.com
Graphic Designer: Joshua Ashley; joshuaashley.com

DEDICATION

In Loving Memory of My Beloved Sister
Lacisha Michelle Lanier ~ 2/11/74 - 8/30/09
I thought it was her mission to write a book about the testimony of her life before she left the earth, but she has passed the torch to me from heaven saying, "Write, my sister, write."

ACKNOWLEDGMENTS

To my son Tyquon M. Jordan...

You've allowed me to experience that indescribable love that a mother has for her child. It's that limitless love that extends beyond the borders of the earth, and goes throughout eternity. Because of you, I've learned how to love myself and to strive to be a better person, so that I can love and care for you adequately. You were the driving force that allowed me to rededicate my life to God for His guidance, as He entrusted your life into my hands. For it was after I gave birth to you that I realized that God had so much more in store for the both of our lives. I decided to go to hair school and maintained a 21-year career in the beauty industry that has sustained us thus far. You are my inspiration to step out of my comfort zone of doing hair only, and embark upon a career of writing, so that you will know that nothing is impossible if you believe and work hard to fulfill your dreams.

To my dear mother Carolyn Lanier ...

You've poured your love upon me from the moment I entered into this world. I love you with all of my heart. You've raised my four sisters and I in the fear and admonition of the Lord and taught us to love and respect everyone genuinely. You have been and will always be my rock. As I've watched you struggle to raise us, I drew from your strengths as well as your weaknesses. For in watching your strengths, you taught me to always remain humble "for every good and perfect gift comes from God," and without him I am nothing (James 1:17). I've learned in watching your weaknesses to always rely on God for strength, "for His strength is made perfect in our weakness" (2 Cor. 12:9). You taught me, whether weak or strong to always rely on the Source (God) for everything I need in this life.

To my four sisters...

You all have always had my back. I'll love you for all of eternity. The bond that we formed as siblings, going through our struggles together, can never be broken. We have learned to laugh our way through our sadness and to smile - even with tear-glazed eyes. Know that, "Weeping may endure for a night but joy cometh in the morning." I want to declare that morning is here, so let the darkness of our past be washed away by the joy of the light of a brand new day. Let us continue to pour our love on one another. The sky is the limit, so let us shoot for the heavens and fulfill our dreams.

CHAPTER ONE

Water surrounded me. Fear engulfed me.

As I sat on top of the car with my son, in fear that we would be swept away by the rising flood waters, my mind drifted back to the many eleventh hour moments that I had experienced in my life. Those moments when I was in dire need of being rescued and it seemed there was no help in sight. They are called eleventh hour moments, when your back is up against a brick wall, and there is no way out but to go through the many challenging obstacles of life by plowing forward, which may seem impossible to do at the time.

My life had been filled with storms. One after another for as long as I could remember.

There is a saying, "desperate times calls for desperate measures." Where had the days gone when a problem would arise, and the answer to that problem would arrive quickly rather than never, then one's weary mind could finally find rest? Those days seemed to have vanished in the darkest and coldest of the nights of despair, that taunted the minds of those who sought resolution to the problems that had taken root in one's nerve endings. That constant nagging and aggravating pain that was a constant reminder that the problems of life had not gone away, but had taken long term residency. My soul and every ounce of my being screamed out for relief, but relief seemed to have taken an express flight far away from the agonizing pain and misery of my very being.

A raging anger gripped the very pit of my stomach. Bitter by the fact that I had watched others being rescued but the boat had passed right by me numerous times. My mind shouted out, "LET GO…you can't take it anymore!" Then my body began to follow its order of command. I could feel my hands as they began to slip, my legs started to release and my body began to drift. I had completely let go, as my mind commanded me to. I drifted, though I didn't fall. I finally could feel relief for the first time in a while. I was in a state of total peace and serenity. When I opened my eyes I realized that I wasn't drifting, but being carried.

How majestic is the gentle grip of the hand that held me tight, not causing any bodily harm as He carried me away from the raging sea of life-tossed problems and circumstances. It reminded me of how King Kong could climb the highest skyscraper to bring his beautiful prized possession to safety, without a scratch on her body, nor a hair on her head harmed. Of course, that was a fictional movie, but at the same time I always wondered about the mystery of how it was done.

I was carelessly sailing in the hands of my Majestic King. The breeze of the wind wiped away the moisture from my tear-filled face. The brilliance of the light of the One who held me closely, caressed and kissed my face, finishing the job of the wind, and wiped every tear from my eyes. I wanted to ask Him, "Why did you wait so long to come?" Yet, my mouth would not dare form to utter a single word. So I held my peace, as the feeling of peace invaded every ounce of me. The One who carried me, began to speak to me without saying a word. Somehow, the communication was through our connected hearts that beat together, creating a language that was not audible but which I clearly understood.

His thunderous heartbeat spoke softly to me, and the first words He spoke were, "I love you."

I could feel my tear ducts trying to formulate more tears, but their reservoir of water had run dry. Perhaps I had run out of tears, all cried out by life's disappointments and failures. Or perhaps the One who wiped them away, sealed them tightly by the tender kisses of His love and said, "No more tears for now."

My battered and bruised heart spoke softly back to Him and said, "Oh, how I love you, too!"

Just then, I could feel Him touching my broken heart, putting it back together again. As He repaired each section, the memories of different heartbreaks flashed before my eyes, then suddenly disappeared, then the pain of it vanished for good.

I looked and the bruises were gone and my heart was suddenly whole. I then fully could embrace the power of His love, that rushed in like the water of a broken levee, invading the homes that are in its path. My body became limp, fully succumbed to His love. So I totally surrendered and took it all in.

That temporary state of euphoric peace that I felt, soon faded away that day on top of the car. And I began to blame myself for being in that predicament, for not listening to the voice of my mother. Just days prior to the storm hitting landfall, my mother harassed me constantly to leave the city of Houston to avoid the flooding. My mother's voice was like a smoke detector when its battery was no longer working. It was a constant chirping that aggravated me to my very core.

Being born and raised in Springfield, Massachusetts, the words hurricane and flooding would horrify and melt our snow-filled hearts.

Hurricane Harvey was scheduled to hit landfall on Friday, August 26, 2017. However, Houston was not expected to get a direct hit. Therefore, we were not under a mandatory evacuation. I tried to reassure my mother that the storm was not going to be that bad.

"Look, Mommy, you are really overreacting," I told her. "I've been living in Houston for a little over twelve years now, and every time we've had a mandatory evacuation, I have left town," I said, trying to convince her that her gut feeling was totally wrong. I continued to school her about the nature of hurricanes as if I were a meteorologist and knew what I was really talking about.

"Whole cities never flood! When we watch the news and they show the devastation of a city due to a hurricane or tornado or whatever storm they are covering, they make it seem as if the whole city is completely under water." I continued to take my mother to my bootlegged school of meteorology. "For instance, with Hurricane Katrina..."

I had just moved to Houston on June 27, 2005, only two months before Hurricane Katrina had hit. The torrential rainfall from Katrina, put excessive weight on the levees, which are floodgates to hold back the water because the city of New Orleans was built below sea level. With an already breached levee system, it gave out, and the city did not stand a chance. It was one of the biggest disasters in U.S. history. Its catastrophic flooding subdued the city after the storm was over, causing over 1,800 flood-related deaths in the city of New Orleans.

Further schooling her, I said "... the news made it seem like all of New Orleans was totally under water."

By this time, I needed some class participation from an unconvinced student.

"Mommy, isn't that right... you thought that the entire city was completely under water?"

My mother very slowly and cautiously answered me, "Well from what I saw on the news, yes it did seem like the entire city was flooded out."

I slowly pulled my mother into my net of convincing her that I was right, like a big fish that latched onto the bait. Just before that fish could fully taste the shrimp, he was reeled in and plopped into a net before he was fully aware of what happened.

"See? I will be okay! And furthermore, I live in a two story house with an attic, and even if the water comes in, and trust me it will not, I could retreat to the attic," I said.

My mother paused for a brief moment to process the information I had given her. She abruptly said, "Well do you have an ax to chop through the roof, just in case the water comes up to the second floor, and you become trapped?"

I laughed hysterically at my mother's comment and said, "Mommy, me and Ty are going to be just fine!"

So I thought.

Regret filled me as I sat on the car. Why did I not take the warning of my mother's frantic voice telling my son and me to get out of harm's way seriously? If anything happened to my son, I would've never forgiven myself. Or better yet, if we both perished, I would've closed my eyes restlessly and been haunted beyond the grave. I would have definitely taken the hit for that one. I have often taken on the blame for a lot of things in my life.

Being the fourth child of the five daughters my mother had, I was blamed for plenty of things that I did not do. My older sisters knew my youngest sister was far too young to blame for the many miscellaneous screw-ups around the house, so I was next in line to take the brunt of the blame. I was old enough to understand what was going on, but not quite old enough to properly defend myself.

I'd often sit in fear as my mother would demand to know why I'd done something that my sisters had blamed me for. On the witness stand, unable to plead my case to the prosecution, which were my three older sisters at the kitchen table, and my mother, the judge asking me, "Well did you do it? Speak now or forever hold your peace!" Silence and fear would clutch my voice box, and not a word would escape to declare my innocence.

All three of my older sisters would shout to the top of their lungs, "Yes, Ruby did it."

I was guilty as charged because I didn't open my mouth to defend myself. The verdict was finalized and the judge, my mother, did the sentencing. It was the end of a belt or a phone cord to connect to my backside. With every syllable she spoke to chastise me, the tool of punishment came crashing down on my flesh. My fear of beatings caused me to fall out on the ground and breakdance, as my mother fought hard to aim the belt to land on my butt. She would often miss the aimed target as I squirmed and twisted, and rolled like an urban dance group out on the street dancing with a piece of cardboard underneath their feet, to a fast-paced rhythm. I would pop, lock, and roll, as I tried my best to avoid the constant swinging of my mother's arm, and whatever tool of punishment she chose for that day. Some days she would grab whatever was closest to her. It could be a hanger, a house slipper, or even a shoe. From the outside looking in, someone might have thought it was child abuse, but that wasn't the case at all. It was just the case of a single mother, frustrated, struggling to raise five children on her own. She refused to tolerate any more disrespect, that is, after she left our father.

Our father abused and disrespected our mother on a regular basis, often beating her senseless. He made her feel worthless, and less than human. He treated her like her only purpose on earth was to serve him, and to take whatever cruelty that he dished out to her.

There were many nights that the horrifying screams of my mother would often wake my sisters and me out of our sleep, and the crashing and rumbling of the furniture being moved and broken, as my father tossed my mother around like a lifeless rag doll.

I can remember all five of us laying in the bed with the covers pulled over our heads, screaming and crying helplessly, all while praying, as one does when bunkering down while awaiting a tornado to pass over them, and then the dust to settle.

One night, after such a rambunctious episode, my mother's screams suddenly went silent. We held our breath, hoping that there was still life in her body. The silence was then broken by the whimpering of my mother's faded cry, and her pain-filled prayers, crying out to God in agony.

The back door slammed so hard that I was sure it was going to bounce off the hinges as my demonized father retreated to escape hearing my mother praying, and singing songs of worship to God, in spite of her pain and discomfort. My sisters peeked out, watching him get into his car and drive off, then all five of us rushed to our mother's side to try to help soothe her discomfort. We hugged her, kissed her, and wiped the tears from her eyes.

I despised my father for the way he abused us and my mother. I had vowed that I would never let a man put his hands on me, and especially without giving him a fight. And honestly, I was silently mad at my mother for not fighting back. My sisters and I would have felt much better if my mother would have landed one good punch on him, to make him think twice before he laid another hand on her. Her reluctance to fight back made her an easy prey for him to take out his frustration after a long day at work, after marching to the beat of the drum of his superiors.

That night, as I attempted to soothe my mother's wounds, I finally worked up enough nerve to ask her, "Mommy, why don't you hit him back?"

My mother closed her eyes and tears began to roll down her swollen and bruised cheeks, and into the corners of her bleeding lips. I watched the tears roll from the corner of my mother's mouth, down to her chin, and plop onto her blouse. I jumped up, ran to the restroom, wet some toilet paper in cold water and raced back to place it against my mother's face.

My mother gently took the tissue from me, then took a

deep breath and began to talk.

"Babies, I am so sorry that y'all have to watch your father beat on me..." She paused, fighting back another round of tears, "... but it was not always this way."

"Mommy, what do you mean?" I asked.

She looked from me to my sisters. "Before I had y'all, me and your father used to go toe-to-toe. He would hit me, and I would hit him right back. I would even pick up whatever I could find, and try to knock the cow walking pee out of him."

There were times when my mother's native Pembrooke, Georgia sayings would come out as she scolded us, and we fought hard not to burst out laughing.

But laughter was far from us that day.

"So what happened to you then?" one of us asked. "Why did you stop fighting him back?"

The next words that came out of my mother's mouth, subconsciously was the start of me taking on the blame and guilt of a whole lot of things in my life.

She said, "Well, I put up my boxing gloves for y'all kids."

My heart dropped as my mouth followed its' actions. I whispered, "Mommy, what do you mean?"

She sighed. "I love y'all so much, that I was afraid if I kept on fighting him, that one day I would kill him." She then took a very deep breath and exhaled slowly. "I knew that with my mama being dead, his mother would end up raising y'all, while I served a life sentence for murder."

I'm not sure which terrified me most, my mother confessing that she had the capability to kill someone, or the fear of living with my father's mother, who was twice as ruthless and cruel as he was.

My young mind tried to process what my mother had told

us. I came to a conclusion that her love for us, and concern about our well-being, caused her to accept mistreatment and abuse from our father, not knowing it was killing us silently as we watched.

One day, my sisters and I awakened to the sound of a woman screaming hysterically outside. We ran to the window to see what was going on, and we witnessed my mother and my oldest sister running hand-in-hand down the street, with only the clothing on their backs. Both had looks of terror on their faces. Instant fear had gripped the four of us and I knew I was thinking the same thing as my sisters: Our mother had left us for good, to escape the endless torture of my father's wrath.

I watched with mixed feelings. Part of me was cheering, "Run, mommy," afraid that my father would pursue them and drag them back to the house of heartache and despair, with an iron hook encased around their necks, while they were kicking and screaming and fighting for their lives. I wanted to shout for joy that my mother and sister would no longer have to endure the unbearable pain and misery that saturated their souls under my father's cruel dominion. However, the other half of my mind began to cry out in fear of what would become of the rest of us? With my mother being gone, our check-ups would probably become more often. Every time my mother left to go to the grocery store or run an errand, my father would give us our "Well Children's exam."

As long as I could remember, it was the normal routine to bring all five of us into his bedroom. Then, starting from the youngest to the oldest, our father would make us undress down to our bare bottoms, and lay naked on his bed. We would be on our backs, our legs opened wide, as he opened up the lips of our vagina for a thorough examination.

I remember my father examining me as my oldest sister, Lakeisha, stood there crying, with a look of disgust, fear, and utter helplessness on her face. She watched what were the beginning stages of the sexual abuse she had already endured for years, transpiring before her eyes. She wept for her younger sisters, for she knew that it wouldn't be long before our innocence would be snatched away.

That was our routine while we lived with our father. He said that he had to check to make sure everything was well, and we weren't sick.

In my young and innocent mind, I would compare it to how a doctor tells you, "Open up wide and stick your tongue out," so that he can stick that long wooden stick far down the back of your throat, that causes you to gag as he shines the light down there, to give a thorough examination.

My father's examination was a little uncomfortable, but I was not yet old enough to know that my father's behavior was wrong. Lakeisha's heart bled for all of us, while the rest of us were totally oblivious to the danger that we were in. Our father would often give her a harsher treatment, and at the time, none of us understood why. We were all physically and emotionally abused, but it seemed as though Lakeisha had a hidden target on her back.

There were times when we were all screaming in horror, while watching my mother be pulverized by my father. He would yell, "Shut up!" as we cried and screamed, pleading for him to stop hitting our mother.

For a moment, we thought that he took heed of our pleas, and he'd finally let up off my mother. Then, like a raging bull, he'd charge over to my oldest sister, and with all of his might, his big heavy hand would come crashing down on her face, knocking her to the floor.

As a child I thought Lakeisha got the worst of the mistreatment by my father because she was the oldest and could take the bulk of the burden. I soon learned that wasn't the case.

My mother was seven months pregnant with my oldest sister, when she met my father. He was a high school Spanish teacher who worked at my mother's high school, so he was fully aware of her circumstances prior to him showing any interest in her. My mother had low self-esteem due to the ongoing sexual abuse that she encountered as a child. She was love-deprived and needed a remedy to the pain that oozed from her broken heart. She longed for someone to love her and her unborn child, and to protect them from the wolves that tore her innocence away. My mother and Lakeisha's father's relationship ended shortly after her pregnancy. He was immature and not nearly ready to settle down with anyone, neither was he ready to be a responsible father.

That's the reason why my mother thought when she met my father, she had found her knight in shining armor, as he took interest in her when he saw her going to class. After they exchanged numbers in passing, they began dating. He showed my mother that he was mature and financially stable enough to care for her and her unborn child. To top it all off, he was easy on the eyes. His jet-black afro, made him stand a few inches taller than he actually was. His thick, and perfectly squared off eyebrows, carefully encased his dark brown intense eyes. His goatee wrapped around his medium-sized lips like a custom made leather jacket. He had a smile that lit up the room. His white and bright, flawlessly square teeth would push his cheeks up to the top of his face, causing his eyes to almost disappear when he smiled or laughed, prompting his dimples to suddenly appear. My mother thought she was about to live her life as if it were a fairytale, and live happily ever after. She thought that the pain of her past was over, and that God had given her another chance to experience love. That twinkle in her eyes soon turned into sorrow and tears, as the man who she thought was her knight in shining armor, became her darkest of nights and the start of her endless sorrows.

Minutes seemed like hours as we held our breath, waiting and hoping that our mother and sister would soon return. I ran into the closet, as I heard the voice of my enraged father calling each of our names, "Vanessa, Gail, Ruby, get down here!"

Juanita was our baby sister, so he didn't bother to include her in on whatever task he was getting ready to ask us to do. We walked shaking and trembling in fear, as one on death row walks to their lethal injection chamber. We slowly walked down the long gloomy hallway, down the creaky old staircase, through the kitchen and into the living room to await our sentencing.

We all held our breath and waited for our father to release the lethal gas. Tears filled our eyes from the fumes of his fury, ignited from simply being in his presence, and of course, the fear of the unknown.

He looked at my two older sisters. "Write out all of your multiplication tables, from one all the way up to twelve." He turned to me. "You work on your penmanship."

We all exhaled a sigh of relief, and raced back upstairs

before he changed his mind. As I began to write, I couldn't help but think why in the world he would have us doing schoolwork at a time like *this*.

I became infuriated with my father, as I wrote my name over and over again. I broke the tip off the pencil and my anger was quickly interrupted by a knock on the door. While I could hear them, the knocks were soft at first, but then grew louder.

Finally, my father bellowed, "Who is it?"

By this time, the rest of my sisters had stopped writing their multiplication tables, and listened attentively to learn who was knocking at the door.

"It's the police, open up!" a voice boomed from the other side of the door.

I wanted to scream, "Help us! We're upstairs." But not only was I paralyzed with fear, the police had never helped us before, so I had no confidence that they'd do so then.

Once, a neighbor had heard my mother's screams from across the street and called the police to come to her rescue. By the time the police had gotten there, my mother answered the door with bruises all over her arms. We all stood right next to our mother as they questioned her. In my young mind, I was hoping they would put the bad guy in the police cruiser, never for any of us to see him again. My over 250-pound father, stood tall on top of the hill of our yard, mowing the lawn in blue jean overalls, and a white wife-beater tank underneath it, looking totally unconcerned at the cop car sitting at the bottom of the hill, and the cops talking to my mother while we stood beside her. He continued to mow the lawn as if he had not a care in the world. Both of the officers observed my father briefly as he pushed the lawn mower in front of him. They glanced at my mother and asked, "Ma'am... are you married to him?"

My mother's voice was soft and low as she replied, "Yes I am."

The next words that came out of one of the officer's mouth that day, is what made me question if they ever would be able to help me and my three sisters.

The officer told my mother, "Then there is nothing we can do about it. We are sorry, but we can't help you."

My mouth fell open as I watched the police car fade away in the distance. My memory of the police's past failure to help my mother was interrupted by a series of even more intense knocking than before, followed by the repeated words, "Open up!"

By this time, we all ran to the window of our bedroom. It was the same window that we all ran to when we heard the screams of our frantic and panicked mother, running down the street with my sister hand-in-hand like runaway slaves, heading toward the north to find their freedom. The intensity was real. When we peered outside, we saw my mother with the police, standing at the door, and our sister standing across the street with one of my uncles. My mother did not abandon us after all! She just left to get some reinforcements so that we could leave my father without him doing any further damage to her or us.

Seeing my mother at that moment, was better than the feeling of seeing all the beautifully wrapped gifts under the tree with my name written on them on Christmas morning. Our fears and uncertainties turned into joy as the officers escorted my mother into the house to retrieve us and a few of our belongings. My mother declined to take any of the material things from the house.

"All I want are my babies out of there. He can have everything," she said.

The tears flowed from all of our eyes as we hugged and embraced our mother. The officers said that they had to ask each of us individually who we'd want to stay with, our mother or our father. With no hesitation we all cried out, "Mommy, we want to go with you!"

Although my baby sister was just short of four-years-old at the time, she had enough sense to know that it was beyond time to go. She clung to my mother's ankles and said, "Mommy, I want to leave."

My mother picked her up and held her so tightly and cried tears of relief. I learned later in life, why my mother had to retreat with my oldest sister, with only the clothing on their backs without the rest of us. On that dreadful day, my mother walked in on my father molesting my oldest sister, he was having full-fledge intercourse with my twelve-year-old sister. My mother found out that it had been going on from the time my sister was four-years-old. This nearly killed my mother, and almost caused her to lose her mind, because she had known all too well the devastating and long lasting effects of sexual abuse. She had purposed in her heart she would protect her children from child predators. She never wanted any of her children to have to suffer in silence as she did when she was a child. She knew that she had to lean on something that was more powerful than any earthly being, to get her through the devastation of what she and her children had gone through.

My mother continued to turn to God for help to get her through the very long days ahead of her, so that she and her children could heal properly.

My mother stood up and raised her hands in praise as tears gushed from her eyes. One of the sisters from the small Pentecostal church poured out all of her heart and soul as she sang her own rendition of Psalms 121. All five of us sat next to our mother, and clapped our hands as the passionate song leader began to chant the main chorus to the song.

"Help is on the way," she sang.

The lady leading the song motioned for the congregation to join in with her as she continued singing.

"Help is on the way."

Soon, the entire church, including my mother and all five of us were singing along. I could tell the words touched my mother's broken and bruised soul. She had searched for help for years, and there was no help in sight. This song was right on time to encourage and give my mother hope, that her rescue was finally in progress for herself and her five babies. Her weary soul and mind could finally receive rest from the torment of guilt that tried to stain her mind and soul.

She did not know how her help was coming, but she knew according to the song, where it would come from. She received the assurance that she was forgiven by God when she walked to the front of the church to rededicate her life to God.

That alone gave my mother the strength to keep on moving forward.

CHAPTER TWO

"Mom. Mom! Come on, we have to keep moving. Or they'll never see us in here."

The voice of my son quickened my mind back to the current crisis at hand.

"What are you doing?"

"Mom, we have to get out of here!"

My nerves were racing as I ran to the master bedroom and jerked open the cabinet, looking for some type of tool or device to be able to cut through the roof to avoid going out into the flood waters. I grabbed the hammer and a box cutter, and pulled down the latch to the attic to see if I would be able to cut my way through there.

My son trailed behind me as I tried to hammer the ceiling of my attic to break to the roof. I summoned every ounce of strength as I crashed the hammer into the top of the ceiling hoping to get some penetration.

Again and again. My heart quickened with every pound.

"I can't swim," I muttered. *We can't die,* I thought.

But despite my best efforts, it barely buckled. Still, I was a mad woman as I slammed the hammer over and over again, and began to yell at the ceiling, as if it would obey my commands.

"Come on you stupid ceiling, open up so we can get out of here.... I'm not playing with you! Open up!"

"Mom, it's not working," my son cried.

The desperation in his voice made me try to think of other options.

"I know what we can use," I said as I ran into my son's room and grabbed his college futon. I pulled it out so that we could use it as a floating device. I snatched the fitted sheet off his bed and tied it tightly around my waist. My son could no longer hold his peace and asked, "What are you doing with that?"

I quickly answered, "It's for you to hold the other end. Just in case I slip under the water, you'll be able to pull me back in."

Tears filled my son's eyes as he fought hard to prevent them from escaping. My son had always felt the pressure to be the man of the house. It was a pressure that I had worked hard never to put on him. But I believe many young men raised by single mothers, form a very special bond with their mothers, and eventually take on the burden that their mothers carry. They then become resentful towards their absentee fathers, for them not helping alleviate some of the pressure off of their mothers. Then once they come into early manhood, they feel a sense of obligation, or even possibly indebted to us for taking care of them. My son had felt that pressure like never before. His birthday was right around the corner, and he would legally be considered a man.

I don't know why, but my mind went back to a time when my son had called me from his dorm room, upset and frustrated because of an unexpected outstanding balance for his college tuition. The balance was over seven thousand dollars, and had taken me by surprise, too.

"Mom, I'm going to quit college to get a job, because you shouldn't have to carry the load of my tuition and all of the bills by yourself," he said.

"Son, a black man without an education in this world doesn't stand a chance," I told him, before adding, "and just so you know, not finishing college is not an option. It's not a burden for me to work hard for you to be able to fulfill your dreams."

My son had just transferred from a junior college to a private university. His dream was to be a college basketball player, and then go pro. I had always instilled in my son that he could be anything that he wanted to be, except a failure.

"The only way one fails in life is to give up on one's dreams, or in what one believes in. For without belief, one is lost before he is ever found," I often told him.

My son had never played organized basketball prior to the eighth grade. He tried out to play in the seventh grade and didn't make the team. Shortly after, he suffered a hip injury while leaving the nurse's office after he pulled his groin while playing kickball during gym time. The nurse had given him an ice pack, and he laid down for a few minutes. He was unaware that the janitor had just mopped the office floor. They failed to put a wet floor sign down, and he slipped and fell in the most awkward way. Both of his legs flew from underneath him, and his left leg twisted and bent behind him, and he landed flat on his back. The force of the fall, chucked a piece of bone from his hip area, about the size of a quarter. The doctor was straightforward about the seriousness of his injury, and how important it was for him to heal properly.

"If it doesn't heal properly, you might not be able to

function as a normal child, or be involved in physical activities such as sports," the doctor warned. "Stay completely off the hip so you don't injure it any further and have to have hip surgery. If you require surgery, you most likely will never play sports again."

So my son took to bed rest. I even had to purchase a bedpan for him to release his waste. I also had to sponge bathe him because he was not permitted to stand, not even to shower. The doctor said that the bone would eventually fill back in on its own as long as he stayed off of it.

My son went from bed rest, to a wheelchair for three months. The stress and pressure weighed heavily on me as a single mother trying to take care of a once-fully functioning child, to a disabled child, and it seemed unbearable at the time. The pressure to make sure that he healed properly came crashing down on me like a malfunctioning crane. It almost killed me to see how depressed my son had become as he tried to maneuver his way around in a wheelchair. It was one of the most difficult times of our lives.

To make matters even worse, when he returned to school, I had to sign my son into the office every morning, while the office staff acted as if I was the cause of his injury. They held a personal grudge against me because I dared question how he could be hurt at school. Of course, it hadn't helped that I had completely lost my cool the day he was injured and they sent him home on the bus, barely able to walk because the pain was so intense.

He was barely shuffling his feet to walk when I met him at the bus stop. So after I brought him to the emergency room that day and I saw the missing bone from my son's hip on the x-ray, I made a visit to the school the next day to get all of his assignments, as well as give the administration a piece of my mind for sending my son home with a broken hip. Instead of them putting themselves in my shoes and empathizing with my pain and frustration, they judged me as just another angry black woman, and not a concerned mother.

After three long and painful months, my son's days of being bound to a wheelchair had come to an end. He moved to crutches, then after eight weeks of being on crutches, the doctor allowed him to walk with no assistance, though his activities were limited.

The doctor slowly approved no-impact activities such as swimming to get him fully mobile again. By the summer going into his eighth grade year of school, he was able to play the sport that he loved and missed dearly. He made a full recovery without the need for surgery.

I thank God for his full recovery and giving me the strength to care and provide for him, and for giving the doctors the knowledge to instruct me on how to do so.

As a single and working mother, I never really had the time, nor the money to expose my son to the whole organized basketball arena that most kids were exposed to such as AAU (Amateur Athletic Union). However, in spite of his limited experience playing organized basketball and his hip injury, he played basketball all four of his high school years. He started on the freshman "A" team his first year, which was the more advanced team out of the two freshman teams that they had. For his sophomore year, and throughout his senior high school basketball career, he played on the varsity team. He was voted MVP for both of his junior and senior years at his high school. He won awards for district and regional basketball tournaments. His senior year, his basketball team made it all the way to regionals, and lost in double overtime to make it to the state tournament. It was the farthest his team had gone since 1946.

With his record, I was sure I wouldn't have to pay for his college education. Boy, was I wrong. We struggled to find him a college that would offer a scholarship. There were Division 2 and 3-level colleges that wanted him to play for them, but they offered little to no money. I didn't want to lock him into a four-year college that wasn't the college of his choice, and still have the tuition come out of my pocket. We then decided to have him go to a junior college in Dallas. That was another difficult task because although my son was an excellent basketball player, he had an unorthodox way that he played, because he was not trained to play organized ball.

When my son was a little boy, I would bring him to the local parks to shoot around with him. He always had a natural ability to make the shot at an early age. We would play one-on-one, and I would have no mercy on him.

"Come on, Mom, that's not fair," he would whine as I stole the ball from him.

I told him, "Life is not fair, so you have to hold on to what you love."

I would frustrate my son to the point of tears and he would attempt to forfeit the game. I would trail behind him as he pouted off and sat down, nearly out of breath as he grabbed for his jug of water. As he pouted, I would proceed to give him a pep talk.

"Oh, so are you just going to sit down and cry now, or are you going to get up and take back what is rightfully yours?" I asked.

He would often stare straight ahead as if no one was sitting beside him. He would put the nozzle of the gallon of water to his mouth, and begin to down the water like a camel in the desert.

"So are you just going to give up?" I asked during one of his pouting sessions.

This time, he took a big gulp of water and answered, "No, I was just taking a rest."

I nodded, pleased with his answer. "It's all right to take a quick rest in life to catch your breath, because some things in life can knock the wind out of you. But after you have caught your breath, you have to get up and keep on going. Do you hear me?"

He paused, then turned to me. "Yes mom, I hear you."

I smiled and said, "Great, then let's go play some ball!"

CHAPTER THREE

"Come on, son...we have to go!" I told my son as he grabbed a few of his belongings and threw them in a small plastic trunk.

With the fitted sheet wrapped around my waist, I pushed my son's futon down the stairs. It slid down quickly, and then crashed into the wall on the landing. I then kicked it down the lower flight of stairs and it floated in the water that had begun to fill the lower level of the house. I firmly grabbed onto the railing, in an attempt to detach the railing off of the staircase. My hope was to use it as a paddle to maneuver the futon. But the railing was tightly bolted down, and I couldn't get it off.

"Mom, time is wasting, we don't need that," my son said as he waded into the water and took the other end of the futon. "Come on, follow me outside," he said, extending his hand.

At that very moment I realized that the seed that I had cared for and cultivated for years, had fully bloomed and was providing fruit and shade for me, too. It was at that moment when the student became the teacher, the mentee became the mentor, the boy became a man.

Fear had invaded my soul, but I took comfort as my six-foot-three-inch son beckoned for me. With the end of the sheet that was tied tightly around my waist, I placed the end of the sheet in his hand. He wrapped it around his hand a few times, and held it securely along with the handle to the plastic trunk that held his personal belongings. I walked down the stairs as a new Christian walks down the stairs and into the baptism pool. Once we made it to the door, my son unlocked it and attempted to open it, but it wouldn't budge. He readjusted the locks in frustration to make sure they all were unlocked.

"Let me try," I said.

I made sure that all three locks were opened on the door, and tugged real hard, but the door still wouldn't budge.

"I think the water pressure on both sides of the door has it jammed," I said. "It's going to take a team effort and the help of God to open the door. On the count of three, we are both going to pull on the door with all of our might."

He nodded and grabbed the doorknob with me.

"Ready? One…two…three!"

We jerked as hard as we could and the door slammed opened with a forceful hit, and the water rushed in, knocking us both back.

This can't be happening, I thought as the water rapidly rushed in. I fought to hold my breath.

I could hear my son yelling, "Mom, where are you?"

I wanted to answer but I couldn't. I was fully submerged as the force of the water pushed me back toward the door. I managed to get my head above water and gasped to take a breath. I realized I'd been knocked over, so I stood, took another quick breath, and then the waves came and swept me off my feet again.

Overcome by panic, I just knew it was over, as the water surrounded me. I couldn't think clearly enough to find my way back on my feet. But then…I felt arms wrap around me.

"Mom, hold on. I got you!"

My son had me around the waist and had somehow managed to pull me up and onto the futon. I coughed uncontrollably, as I tried to catch my breath.

"Mom, are you okay?" my son cried.

I nodded in between coughs and managed to give him a weak 'thumbs up.'

With the little strength I had left, I pulled the rest of my body onto the futon. My coughing subsided as the water made its escape from my lungs.

Finally, I said, "Son, I'm okay now."

A look of relief filled my son's eyes when he heard my exhausted voice.

He said, "Mom, just lay here, I'm going to walk the futon outside, so that we can be rescued."

I nodded my approval, as he stood in front of the futon and began to push it out of the door.

I gasped at the sight of my neighborhood. It looked like it had been built in the middle of a lake. I looked to the left of me, my son's car was halfway submerged under the water. Sorrow and sadness filled my soul.

Since we didn't know how bad it was beyond what we could see, we decided not to go any further.

"Let's wait on top of the car for a rescue boat to get us," I told my son.

He nodded in agreement, then pushed the futon all the way up to the car, and I climbed on top of the car. My son then climbed onto the car with me and we waited to be rescued. We watched the futon float off. As it drifted in the distance, my mind began to drift to a moment in time.

I was a seventeen-year-old girl, pregnant and scared. "How did I get myself into this predicament?" I'd often ask myself. I was raised in the home of a strict Christian mother. My mother took my sisters and me, to a small Pentecostal church that she attended, so I knew that fornication was wrong. I was not even promiscuous. I fought long and hard not to indulge in the forbidden fruit of intimacy, even though most of my friends had already engaged in sexual activities early on in their teenage years.

Springfield, Massachusetts had very little to offer young people, or any one for that matter. Young men would often succumb to gang violence, and end up locked up, strung out on drugs, or six feet under. While young women would end up pregnant even before they could fully enjoy their teenage years.

I guess boredom, along with being tired of trying to resist the strong sexual feelings that I felt, had finally gotten the best of me after I was exposed to it at an early age. I started having sex only a few months before my seventeenth birthday. I found out I was pregnant, not too long after I turned seventeen-years-old. I had no clue what was going on with me prior to finding out that I was pregnant. I constantly had to go to the bathroom and my appetite had increased like I had a hole in my stomach. I still had no clue that I was pregnant. Although my three oldest sisters already had children, having a child was the last thing on my mind.

One day, I was in the basement doing sit-ups with a 20-pound weight on my stomach. As I was elevating my upper torso to complete the sit-up, my stomach mounted up in the biggest knot that would not leave for about a minute straight. After it went away, I went upstairs to my mother's room and told her that I needed to see a doctor, because I might possibly be pregnant. A look of utter surprise and hurt filled my mother's eyes. This was a hard blow for her. She didn't even suspect that I was sexually active.

My mother's friends and our close relatives would comment, "Is another one of your daughters pregnant?"

They couldn't understand with my mother being strict on us, and keeping us in church, how four out of her five daughters, ended up pregnant out of wedlock. We all were exposed to sex prematurely by a man who should have protected and shielded us from it. All of us were in search for a man to love us long before the time was appropriate.

The day I told my mother that I thought I was pregnant, I immediately considered something that was totally against our Christian beliefs.

"I can have an abortion," I told her, my heart sinking at the mere utterance of those words. I didn't want to be pregnant, but the idea of harming my unborn child tore at my soul.

Without blinking, my mother said, "If you are pregnant, you're going to have the baby."

And that was the end of that conversation.

My mother did take me to the doctor to confirm the pregnancy and the test was positive. I was seventeen and about to be a mother when I was just beginning to have a little bit of fun. New Year's Eve – was the first time I'd ever gotten drunk and the night I believe I got pregnant. My boyfriend at the time, knew I wasn't a drinker or the partying type, so we celebrated the holiday at his apartment having a couple of drinks.

I had gotten in tip-top physical shape. I had a six pack, with a 26" waist, 38" hips, and a 36" bust. Everywhere I went, car horns would blow. Still, I didn't think I was beautiful enough. I would work out seven days a week, for two and a half hours at a time. My fitness was the only thing that I felt I had control over in my life, so exercised obsessively. I guess I was striving for perfection in my appearance to mask all of the hurt and pain of an unstable childhood. Although, that soon changed with my pregnancy.

After we left my abusive father's house, we lived in very unstable situations. The first place we stayed was with my uncle and his wife, and their six children in a three-bedroom apartment. They gladly welcomed all six of us, and tried to accommodate us the best way that they could. However, with the six of us invading their space, there were twelve of us crammed into their small apartment. It wasn't long before we wore out our welcome and the tension began to grow between my uncle's wife and my mother. It wasn't anything major, it was the little petty things that began to eat away at the both of them.

For instance, on my mother's nights to cook, she would cook a full course meal like fried chicken, rice and gravy, green beans, and cornbread. While on some of my aunt's nights to cook, she would scramble up some hamburger meat and pour sauce over it and make us all sloppy joe sandwiches. I loved eating sloppy joe sandwiches, but this got under my mother's skin. She firmly believed in feeding her children a full course meal, even when the cabinets appeared to be bare. She would go into the kitchen and make an abracadabra meal out of practically nothing, and we would be full and satisfied. We were only supposed to be there for a short amount of time. And rightfully so, my aunt had every reason to be aggravated with her living situation.

One day tensions were so high between my mother and aunt, that my mother called my grandfather, and we left my uncle's house that day, and moved in with him. This was the second of many moves we would encounter. I don't think that my mother quite understood how taxing it was for people to take in a family of six. She just wanted people to do the right thing and treat us fairly. But there's only so far that patience will go when you take up the entirety of someone's home.

I often heard my mother quote the lyrics to Billie Holiday's song, "God Bless the Child" in her frustration. She would say, "Momma may have, and daddy may have, but God bless the child that has his own."

My mother soon moved out of my grandfather's house. That was just the beginning of our instability in our education, because with every move came a different school. I attended so many elementary schools, that I lost count of them. It was hard always being the new girl in class. So I remained quiet, and I only spoke when spoken to, as if my quietness would make me invisible. I always had the uncomfortable feeling of butterflies in my stomach while trying to adjust and readjust with the frequent changes in our living arrangements.

I remember the time when my mother had gotten into it with my grandfather's wife, because my oldest sister had gotten into a fight with her granddaughter. My grandfather had married her after the death of my mother's mother, although they had separated long before my grandmother actually died. My cousin, Lena, technically wasn't our blood cousin because her mother was not my grandfather's child. However, my grandfather loved Lena like she was his own flesh and blood. My sister had held out and avoided fighting my cousin, but it was a long time in the making. My cousin was spoiled and always had gotten her way. Whatever she wanted, my grandfather would always find a way to give it to her. She would taunt and agitate us, and my grandfather would constantly stick up for her. I could hear her whining, with her big lips poked out saying, "Grand-dad, Grand-dad, they won't let me play with their toys."

My grandfather would plead with us. "Come on...would y'all please let her play with it for a little while? Y'all have to share."

The problem was, she had a problem sharing her things with us. We couldn't overlook the pity in our grandfather's eyes as he tried to keep the peace in the house between us and his spoiled rotten grandchild. One day, my cousin did the unthinkable, as she put her hand in my oldest sister's plate and took her chicken wing. Lakeisha could no longer take the aggravation and outright disrespect. My sister knocked my cousin to the ground, and grabbed the mop, and literally turned Lena into a push mop as she mopped the floor with her. My grandfather asked no questions and began to scold my sister by backing her up in the corner, yelling at her while shaking his finger in her face. My sister shook in terror, probably having flashbacks to when we lived with our father. Although my grandfather had never laid a hand on any one of us to discipline us, my mother decided to move out anyway.

Our next move was to a government-assisted motel. They

had given us two rooms to accommodate the six of us, with two queen sized beds in each room. However, our mother didn't want to separate us because the motel was pretty unsafe, so we all crammed into one of the rooms. My mother purchased a crock-pot, and a one-eyed burner, so that she could make us a hot meal just about every night.

Although we were sharing one room of a welfare motel, it was the first time that I felt we weren't a bother to anybody. Our next move was with one of the ladies from the church we attended. We stayed there until my mother's Section 8 came through. We then moved into a two-story house. We finally had a place of our own.

However, it was short lived because it was across the street from the cemetery, and it terrified us. We had experienced some paranormal activities there. There were doors leading to the attic that would forcefully fly opened at various times. We'd quickly run downstairs and into our mother's bedroom and dive into the bed with her. When my mother nailed those doors shut and they continued to fly open forcefully, it was time to go. From there we moved to a four-bedroom apartment in the projects, where we lived for eight years. Then, from the projects, we moved to another two-story house. After that, as part of my mother's final divorce decree, they awarded her the house that we had escaped from when we initially left my father many years ago.

My parents had been legally separated for many years, and the divorce was finally finalized. The house was a blessing and a curse at the same time. Although it was paid for, the horrific memories of our past constantly stained our memories in every room. It was the final move before we all moved out and lived on our own.

That's why I thought of abortion in the first place, when I found out I was pregnant. I didn't want to raise up my child to deal with the instabilities that I had to live with throughout my childhood. Financially, I knew that I was in no position to raise a child. I thank God, however, for my mother talking me back to my senses.

My son was truly a blessing to me. He helped to get my life back on track, because I felt the world - with all of its many temptations - pulling on me, and calling my name. When I was five months pregnant, I found out I was having a boy. I knew that I needed to rely on the same type of strength that my mother did to raise five children on her own. I knew that I had to turn to the source of all security, comfort, and strength. I turned to God and recommitted my life to Him about a year after my son's birth.

My son's father and I had definitely grown apart. He simply did not understand my new walk and commitment to Christ. He called himself a five-percenter. Whatever he proclaimed to be, he was never fully dedicated to the cause. One minute he wanted to listen to Louis Farrakhan and wear bow ties and shave his hair close to his head, with a half-mooned shaped part in it. The next minute, he would be cursing me out.

He would sell bean pies on the corner for his Mosque, similar to how churches sell fish dinners to raise money for their building fund, although they never quite raised enough money to actually purchase the building. He would greet every black woman that he approached with, "Hey beautiful black queen, mother of the earth and all things living, would you like to buy a bean pie?"

He'd also call me his beautiful black queen, mother of

the earth, and all things living. One minute he'd praised me for giving him his firstborn son, then the next minute I was called every ungodly name when I wouldn't give into him.

"If you were a real Muslim, you would stop disrespecting me the way that you do," I'd shout out to him.

I was trying to honor my commitment to Christ by abstaining from sex without being married.

"You know another woman will do what you won't," he often told me.

He found that woman. Right in my own household. My cousin that my mother took in and raised from the time that she was six years old, slept with my son's father. There was nothing left in me for him after that, except the fact that we had a son together. He didn't understand my vow of celibacy, but I was serious about it because a year after I had my son, I was pregnant with his second child and miscarried the baby. Before the miscarriage, I had prayed to God that He would take the baby because I was not in the position to raise another child. I already had to take drastic measures to allow the welfare office to keep me on assistance until I finished hair school, as a new rule was set in place that they would not pay for a second child while I went to school. I would have had to quit school to do community service or work an underpaying job to support the second child. And furthermore, I had told my case worker that she would not see my face again in the welfare office, after she basically told me that I would fail trying to pursue a career as a hairstylist.

I had scheduled an appointment for an abortion on a Friday. Three days before my scheduled appointment, I fasted and prayed for God to intervene.

I prayed, *"Father, I know that I don't even deserve to come to you* now. I have strayed and turned my back on you once again. My mother taught me that you don't hear a sinner's prayer. I'm asking you this one time if you would please make an exception. I am in desperate need of your help. Please forgive me of my sins. I'm asking you to take this baby back with you, Lord. However, if you choose not to, please forgive me of what I am going to do on Friday...Amen."

I fasted and prayed for three days straight. It wasn't lost on me that I was asking God to kill the fetus living inside of me. But my back was against the wall, and I didn't want to deal with the guilt that came with having an abortion. I knew that God would forgive me for taking an unborn life through abortion, but the question was, would I have forgiven myself.

Probably not, because I had always taken the blame for things, and always had a hard time letting go of the past mistakes that I had made.

The Thursday afternoon, the day before my scheduled appointment, I went into the bathroom while in school with the worst stomach cramps that I'd ever experienced outside of childbirth. God somehow did hear the cry of a sinner.

I praised and thanked God in the bathroom stall of the beauty school for coming through in the eleventh hour, not even a full day before my scheduled appointment to the abortion clinic.

This testimony is not to inflict guilt on women that choose abortion. God is humanity's ultimate judge. It is God who forgives all sins, that is, if we confess and repent of them. Yes, even abortion. No one should hold their head in guilt if they have had abortions and have repented and asked for forgiveness. I had made a solemn vow to the Lord that I would draw even closer to Him.

I often would beat myself up trying to strive for moral

and spiritual perfection. The Pentecostal church taught as though that could actually be achieved. Although no one is perfect, I fully dove into what the Pentecostal church called living a sanctified lifestyle. After I accepted Christ, I attempted to clean myself up outwardly first, to obtain inner righteousness.

For example, my entire wardrobe changed because as a Pentecostal Christian, I was not permitted to wear pants, nor make-up, or any jewelry. I was wearing long dresses with stockings, and sandals in the summertime. I was trying to achieve holiness or inner spiritual cleanliness by external ritualization and traditions. I was happy at my choice in a closer walk with God, but I was miserable with the way I was forced to look as a young Christian woman. I had always loved fashion as most hairstylists do. I had stripped everything that I loved and that identified me, as me.

I had become the mold of the image of all Pentecostal Christians, and had lost my authentic identity. I know now that my outward appearance had absolutely nothing to do with receiving and maintaining my salvation.

One day when I was arching my eyebrows with my tweezers in the mirror, getting ready for church service, my mother walked in the bathroom and told me that I was arching them entirely too much.

"This is where I draw the line in the sand," I mumbled after she left the bathroom. I had already stopped wearing pants, jewelry, and make-up to comply with what my mother and the Pentecostal church's definition of what being a Christian was all about. I thought to myself, *How unattractive does she want me to become?* I already didn't feel as beautiful as my peers because they were free to express themselves as far as their fashions, jewelry, and cosmetics went. I was not going to walk around with bushy eyebrows to appease the church's stipulations for living a Christian lifestyle. If arching my eyebrows were going to keep me out of heaven, then I would just have to take my chances.

With my newfound commitment of celibacy, and to remain faithful to God, I decided that I would pray for God to send me a husband. I was a young woman, and a single mother with a son to raise. I also had sexual needs that could not be fulfilled outside of the covenant of marriage. I definitely did not want to be one of these women in the church that grew old pretending like all they needed was Jesus, and they didn't need or desire the companionship of a man.

I just knew that I was ready for marriage. I believed that God would grant my heart's desires of wanting a godly husband, because of my commitment to Him. I showed up to every church service, and faithfully paid my tithes every week. I even showed up to some of the early morning prayer services that they had every day, if my work schedule permitted me to do so. I would try to help those in need whenever I could.

CHAPTER FOUR

One Sunday, there was a young man that showed up in the church service that I had never seen before. He caught my attention because he was so clean cut, with nice curly hair. He had perfectly smooth chocolate brown skin and light brown dreamy eyes. His tailor-fitted vest showed off his appealing physique, and hugged his slim waist to perfection. His medium-sized muscular arms shaped and formed the sleeves of his dress shirt and his dress pants accentuated all the right spots. His attire matched from head to toe, and there was not a wrinkle found in it.

He had definitely piqued my interest.

As the service progressed, the pastor's wife stood up to speak.

"I thank God for sending my son to have service with us," she said, motioning toward the handsome man. "I had been fasting and praying for God to save Clayton's soul, and I know that God has heard the cry of a concerned mother. I called his name out last night in prayer, and here he is in church this morning...you can't tell me that God doesn't answer prayers."

All of a sudden his mother had gotten happy while sharing her testimony, and started shouting and dancing with the microphone still in her hand. The organist began to give her some music to match the pace of the beat of her feet. The pastor joined in on his guitar, and the drummer kept up with the beat of her feet, as she picked them up and put them down like she was running a race in place all by herself.

Pretty soon, the whole congregation shared in her excitement, and joined in the praise party with her. Everyone was waving their hands, and jumping for joy, as they did in a good old fashion Pentecostal church service.

After service ended, the first lady introduced her son to me. As we exited, she told me to pray for him so that God would save his soul. I was dedicated to the cause and I prayed for him every morning before I left the house to go to work, and before I laid down to go to sleep. I started off by only praying for him to receive salvation, but then the prayer soon changed to *"Lord, please save his soul, and if it's your will please let him be my husband."*

I should have been praying, *"Lord, give me the husband that you have designed for me."*

I knew absolutely nothing about his personal life, like whether he ever was married, had kids, or if he even had a job or career. All I knew was that I wanted him to be my husband. The men were very scarce in the church I attended. The few that strolled in every now and then were too old or too weird. The pickings were very few, if at all any.

After a while of praying for my pastor's son, I told the first lady that I had developed feelings for him. She told me to just keep on praying, she believed that God was going to do a great deliverance on him. I didn't know what it was that he needed to be delivered from and I didn't really care. I looked at the door of the church every Sunday to anticipate his arrival. Sunday after Sunday I waited. I began to get disappointed because it seemed as if God was not answering my prayers.

A whole year-and-a-half passed and I was starting to think maybe this was not the man that God wanted to be my husband. That determination made me question whether there was a fine line between faith and insanity.

One day as I was leading the congregation in devotional service, my answer to my prayers finally walked through the door. I wanted to leap out of my skin, overcome with joy, but I had to hold my composure.

My sister's eyes met mine, and she looked at me from the congregation. I had moved in with my sister, Gail, after her separation from her daughter's father. She heard me praying night and day, consistently asking for my pastor's son to give his life to Christ, and to be my husband.

Clayton took his seat on the third pew to the far left of the church. I tried not to make eye contact, because I knew that it would throw me off and embarrass me to my core. I also knew that I would melt if I looked into his enchanting light brown eyes. As I went to take my seat after leading the devotional service, Clayton grabbed my hand. He gave me a nod of approval. I was filled with excitement and joy because he acknowledged me.

Pastor took the podium to begin his sermon. "My son had told me that he wanted to sing a sermonic solo, I am asking that he come now," Pastor said.

My gaze followed Clayton to the front of the church. He took the microphone.

"I know that I have been gone from the church for a long time now. You see, I ran away from the church because of some unfortunate things that I had gone through. The church is supposed to be a place where you experience love and God, a place of refuge. But I was hurt in the church as a child and even in my teenage years. So I had decided that I was done with the church, and the world embraced me and showed me more love than the church had showed me. But see, that was a trick of the enemy so that I could stay out in the world, so that Satan could destroy me. I've been out there doing ungodly things, but I could feel God pulling on me, tugging at my heart. I just want to thank my mother for praying for me, and she told me that the saints here are praying for me, so I thank you. Just know your prayers haven't fallen on infertile ground. The song that I am about to sing is, *To the Utmost Jesus Saves.*"

I fought back the tears as I heard his testimony. The year and a half that I spent praying for his soul to be saved, was not time wasted. When he opened his mouth to sing that hymn, I was in awe and amazement with the voice that had come from his lips. The tears rushed from his eyes as he sang with such conviction and sincerity. I could no longer hold back my tears and cried with him tears of joy as I could see God working on his heart.

As he took his seat, the pastor stood up. With tears in his eyes he said, "Thank you, son, for singing that wonderful selection. I want everyone to turn to a very familiar passage of scripture. Would you please turn your bibles to the gospel of Luke, the 15th chapter, verses 11-30. You see, the prodigal son could not clean himself up. 1 John 1:9 says, '*If you confess your sins, he is faithful and just to forgive you of your sins, and to cleanse you from all unrighteousness.*' There are no big or little sins in God's eyes, sin is sin. Just like the prodigal son's father welcomed him home with outstretched arms, the heavenly father would do the same for anyone of us, if we give our lives to Him. You can come back home."

Just then the organist, Clayton's sister, began to play and sing, *Amazing Grace*. The church went up instantly in a praise explosion. The spirit of God saturated the sanctuary. Hands were lifted up in the air as they waved to heaven, while the tears rolled from the eyes of just about everyone in the congregation.

Pastor approached the podium and spoke into the microphone.

"While the spirit is moving, is there anyone who wants to give, or recommit their lives back to Christ? God is calling someone back home. Do not ignore his voice."

My eyes were still closed in worship, but they quickly opened as I heard the explosive roar and applause of the congregation, and my first lady shouting, "Thank you, Jesus" from the top of her lungs, as she jumped up and down for joy.

Clayton was standing at the front of the church with red tear-saturated eyes, as he constantly tried to wipe them from his face. My prayers had been answered right before my eyes. I could no longer hold my composure and began to do a dance of victory that my year-and-a-half long prayer had finally been answered.

Pastor came down out of the pulpit, and stood in front of his son, so that he could repeat the sinner's prayer. After Clayton finished praying with his father, he said, "Welcome home, son." They embraced as tears ran down the both of their faces. Clayton's mother and sister immediately joined them in that embrace.

As I went to greet the first lady as I usually did after every Sunday service, she said "Sister Ruby, there's something that my son wanted to say to you."

My heart was about to beat out of my chest, as I desperately tried to hide just how awfully nervous I was.

Clayton grabbed me by the hand again and said, "Thank you for all of your prayers. My mother told me that you had been praying for me for a while now. I wanted you to know that I could feel your prayers, but I was fighting within myself. However, today was a result of your prayers."

I couldn't say a word. I just nodded my head. It must have looked to him as if I was deaf and mute, as my mind would not let me utter one word.

He said, "I would like to get to know you better, if you don't mind. Here's my number, you can call me anytime."

One word finally escaped from my lips and I said, "Okay."

His mother saw me struggling, trying to form my words, so she interjected and said, "Why don't you take her number so that you can call her, too? Is that okay with you, Sister Ruby?"

I nodded as the word, "Yes," slowly oozed from my lips.

Clayton said, "We'll talk soon."

Almost a month had gone by from the time I had given Clayton my number in church, until the time he actually called. He had not come back to church since then, and I was growing weary and impatient waiting on him to call me.

"I'm about to call him," I told my sister, Gail, one day. "He did give me his number first, and told me to call him."

"No, you are not. Just be patient, he will call you," Gail replied. "Besides you know that Mommy taught us never to chase behind a man. You have done your part. He'll be calling you soon."

I continued to cry out to God in prayer for Clayton, for God to continue to work on his heart. That He would reveal to him that I was to be his wife. I believed with all of my heart that God told me that Clayton was to be my husband. No one could convince me otherwise.

One day my phone rang with an unfamiliar number. I answered anyway.

"Hello, Sister Ruby, this is Clayton."

Excitement completely took over me as I said, "Hello, Clayton. How are you doing?"

I had made up in my mind that the next opportunity I had to talk to him, I would speak in complete sentences.

He answered, "I'm doing fine. I've just been undergoing some major transitions in my life, but you have been constantly on my mind. I've been wanting to call you, but I wanted a fresh start so I changed my number. This is my new number, so please save it."

I replied, "I definitely will."

"I would like to meet up for lunch so that we can talk some more, being that I'm not much of a phone person," he said.

"I would love to," I said, then tried to tone down my enthusiasm so I didn't appear overzealous. "My days off are on Sunday and Monday."

Clayton said, "Then this coming Monday it will be."

"Great. I can't wait so see you. My address is-"

Clayton promptly interrupted me. "Oh, I won't be able to

pick you up."

Bewildered, I paused, then said, "Why not? Is your car being repaired?

"Uh-h, I meant to tell you, that I'm trying to get back on my feet, and I don't have any transportation right now."

"Oh, Clayton, don't worry. I can pick you up, just give me your address," I said.

Clayton gave me his address in Hartford, Connecticut.

I paused again. "I didn't know you live in Connecticut," I said.

"Is that going to be a problem? I'm not really comfortable hanging out in Springfield. I only go there to visit with my parents. I just really started to come back around lately."

I quickly responded, "No. It's not a problem at all!"

Clayton added, "I'll explain some of it to you when I see you on Monday at 6:30pm, after I get off of work."

"Okay. I look forward to seeing you then."

"The same here."

As soon as we hung up, I ran up to Gail and screamed, "I got a date with Clayton on Monday!"

Gail and I embraced as we jumped up and down in celebration. I was so excited that my first date with Clayton was finally planned and about to take place, that I didn't think about the fact that this man was almost ten years older than me, and didn't have any transportation. However, that was the least of my concerns at the time. All I knew was, the answer to my prayers of receiving my husband was finally in motion, and him having no wheels wasn't going to stop it from coming to pass.

The days seemed to drag by as I anticipated my date with Clayton that Monday. I had no idea what to wear? I didn't want to look like I just stepped out of a Sunday morning worship service. I wanted to look sexy, but at the same time sanctified.

The winter months were quickly approaching in Western New England. The air was clear and brisk, and when the wind blew, it gave you the alert that the ground would soon be covered with the brightest and glimmering beautiful white of the first snowfall. I could definitely wear my sexy stiletto leather boots. I wanted to show off my curves, so my sweater dress would hug every curve to perfection. I had the right designer tights to pull together the whole ensemble.

The evening could not come fast enough. My sister had already agreed that she would watch my son for me. I knew that he was in great hands, therefore there would be no pressure for me to rush back. I toiled with the idea of how I would wear my hair. I talked to myself in the mirror, as I tousled my hair back and forth, trying to visualize the perfect hairstyle for the perfect date.

"Maybe I'll wear it down and flowing, with a side part," I mumbled to my reflection. "No, that might be too plain and boring. Perhaps I'll put some twists in the front of my hair, with the back flipped up at the ends. Or better yet, I could show him that I *really* have skills styling hair, if I twist the front of my hair, and spiral-set the back."

Before I had time to make up my mind on which hairdo I wanted, the time had slipped away from me. I only had two hours before my date and an hour of that time would be spent on the highway traveling to get there. I quickly blow-dried my hair as straight as I could. My long black and thick hair felt like silk, as I flat ironed each section. I wanted a little more body, so I took my biggest curling iron, and bumped my hair all over. I shook my head from left to right, making sure my hair swayed effortlessly with the slightest of movement. I called this motion *the body check test*- the sign of a good hairstyle. I had already taken a long bath prior to going to the salon to do my hair. So, all that I had left to do was to run home, throw on my clothes, and give my son a kiss, before I hit the highway to pick up Clayton.

My hair and outfit was on point, and I felt good about my appearance from head to toe. I was running about twenty minutes behind from the time I had set out to leave to make it to Clayton's apartment by 6:30pm. I jumped into my car, and wasted no time trying to make it to my destination. I swerved in and out of lanes trying to make up for lost time. I yelled at the cars in front of me, as I did 85 to 90 miles per hour, on a mission to get to my man. Suddenly the traffic came to a screeching halt. I had to swerve onto the median to avoid slamming into the car in front of me.

I screamed, "No, no, no…this can't be happening right now." I only had 15 minutes left, before I was late getting to Clayton. The traffic looked as if I would never make it there. I tried to call him to let him know that I was stuck in a traffic jam due to an accident, and I would be running a little behind. However, Clayton did not answer his phone. The traffic finally began to let up and I increased my speed significantly to make it there. I made it to Clayton's apartment at 7:05pm. I was 35 minutes late for our first date.

When I pulled up, Clayton was standing on the steps of his apartment, with a look of displeasure on his face. I just knew that his look of frustration would change once he took one look at me. He approached the car, and got into the passenger side.

"Hello Clayton. How are you?"

Clayton rested the back of his head on the headrest and let out a deep sigh. "I'm okay. I'm just tired from a long day of work. I've been standing on my feet all day, and standing outside for an extra 35 minutes didn't help any."

I quickly tried to explain and apologize for my tardiness. "I was running only a few minutes behind trying to get here, and then there was an accident that made me even further behind. I tried to call you so that you wouldn't be waiting on me to-"

Before I could fully complete my sentence Clayton interrupted me and said, "Look, I have a real pet peeve with tardiness. You really need to work on your time management."

My first thought was: *If I didn't have to drive almost a whole hour to pick you up, I would have had plenty of time.* However, I held my peace because I was just so happy to be in his presence. I apologized again for my tardiness, and told Clayton how nice he looked.

His face began to soften up and he said, "Thank you. You look very nice, too. I would like to show you around the city. Hartford has a lot of nice restaurants with great food. What are you in the mood to eat?"

I answered, "I'm not a picky eater at all, and since I'm not familiar with some of the restaurants here in Hartford, you can choose for me."

Clayton answered, "Hey…Since I know my way around the city, it'll be better if I drive. That way we'll make up some of the time that we lost through your tardiness."

I thought: *We lost more time trying to work through your attitude.* However, I didn't say a word. I surrendered the steering wheel, and we exchanged seats.

As Clayton took the driver's seat, he pushed it as far back as it could go. He was about a half inch taller than me, so I thought that the seat adjustment was a little over exaggerated. He adjusted all the mirrors to his liking, grabbed the steering wheel with one hand, and gapped his legs all the way opened like he was carrying a wide load, then he proceeded to take the road. It felt really good for me to be able to sit back and relax, and have a man drive me around for a change.

Once he swerved into traffic, I knew that I was in for a bumpy ride. I quickly grabbed my seatbelt to prepare for the worst. I thought that I had a heavy foot, but Clayton had me beat by a long shot.

"There are some good restaurants near my job at the mall," he said.

"What do you do at the mall?" I asked.

"I work in the women's shoe department in one of the stores at the mall." He answered. He began to explained to me that he was trying to get his life back on track, and make money the legal and honest way.

"There's a lot you don't know about me, but I feel that I could talk to you and it won't go anywhere."

"Sure, Clayton, you can trust me," I replied. "You can talk to me about anything and I promise it won't go anywhere. I have a lot of people that confide in me and I never repeat what they tell me."

"I hope so. I mentioned some things to my family in the past, and the next thing I know, my business is in a sermon or a testimony right after I mention it. I've always felt betrayed. That's part of the reason why I had secluded myself from my family."

I quickly reassured Clayton, "You never have to worry about that with me. You can trust me. I will never betray you."

By this time Clayton had pulled the car into one of the parking spots at the West Farms Mall, and had me on edge wondering what he was about to say. He took a deep breath as he proceeded to reveal to me what seemed like a deep and dark truth about his past.

"I was raised in a church that was somewhat like a cult," he began. "I got called everything except a child of God. So when I was 16 years old, I ran away from home and moved to New York and became a Blood. They accepted and embraced me more than the church did. I sold drugs to make my money, and became hard so that no one would ever take advantage of me again. That scared little boy that people would tease, and call a faggot because of my high pitched singing voice, is gone forever."

I interrupted him, stunned at his revelation. "Church people used to use such a derogatory word on a child? That is so cruel." My heart bled for this now grown man that seemed to revert back to a child in pain, as the tears began to roll from his eyes.

Clayton continued, "Yes, I used to love to sing in the church. But I was often mocked for the wide range, and the extra vibrato that I have in my voice."

I grabbed Clayton by the hand, and reassured him that it would not be that way this time. That he should use his God-given talent to sing in the church, so that he could bless many.

Clayton wiped the tears from his eyes and said, "Maybe you're right. Just maybe I went through all of this so that when I sing, it will be with much more meaning...more anointed."

I answered, "Yes, I know that I really felt it when you sang, *To the Utmost Jesus Saves*, and others did, too. The whole church did."

"Yes, maybe you're right." He looked at me and smiled. "You are just so easy to talk to. Now come on and let's get something to eat. It's getting late, and you have to drive all the way back to Springfield."

"Don't worry about the time. My son is with my sister, and Tuesday's are my lighter days at work."

Clayton said, "Speaking of your son, my mother had mentioned that his father comes to the church often and that he is still really fond of you. That's why I was treading lightly because I don't want to get my feelings involved with you, if you still have feelings for him."

I shook my head. "That chapter of my life is now closed, and has been for a long time. We are not on the same page. Besides that, he slept with my cousin after I decided to fully dedicate my life to Christ. So there is absolutely nothing between us, it's been dead. The only dealings that we have with each other is pertaining to our son."

"Well, that's good to know." Clayton took my hand as we walked into the mall. I felt like a lady, complete and whole for the first time in a long time.

Clayton chose a nice Italian restaurant. It was absolutely beautiful inside. I could see that he had very exquisite taste. A man with a healthy appetite had always been a turn-on for me. Clayton chewed his food, and swallowed it as he licked the remaining sauce from his thick and sexy lips. I got pleasure from watching him devour his entrée. I was lost in his lips, imagining all that he could do with them besides opening them to take his food in.

"Ruby...did you hear me?" Clayton's voice rose, knocking me out of my trance.

"I'm sorry, could you say it again?"

"I am experiencing a lot of financial hardships since I've turned over a new leaf. The commission that I make off selling shoes is not enough. It's just hard right now, because I know where I could make some fast money, and I wouldn't have to struggle anymore."

I interrupted him. "Don't worry about it, Clayton. God is going to honor your faith by you totally relying on Him. He will make a way for you."

Clayton shook his head. "You don't understand, Ruby. It's been very slow, no one's really buying shoes right now. I know the holidays are approaching and the sales will increase with the Christmas and New Year's Eve sales, but my bills are due right now. I didn't have a problem paying my bills when I worked illegally. I may have to move from the apartment that I'm in because I can no longer afford it. I'm embarrassed to say, but I barely have any food in my refrigerator now."

Worry and distress consumed his face. I reassured him once again that everything was going to work out just fine. He looked me in the eyes and said, "You really have a way of making me feel better about my situation. My mother did tell me that you're a woman of faith, and I can feel just by being around you, that she is absolutely right."

The silence of our smiles were broken by the waiter asking us if we needed anything else as she placed the bill by Clayton.

"May I have a to go box?" I asked.

Clayton opened the bill and began studying it like it was a foreign exam. The more he stared at it, I began to feel nervous for him and said, "Hey, Clayton, I'll get it this time. I know that you said that you're going through financial difficulties right now. I'll pay for it. I know that it isn't easy for you trying to get back on your feet."

The tears welled up in Clayton's eyes and rolled down his cheeks. "No one has ever really shown the care that you've shown me in such a short time. Perhaps, you are the angel that God has sent to rescue me out of all of the hurt and pain that I've been through."

Not an angel, just your wife... and you'll find out soon enough, I thought.

By the time we made it back to his apartment, I was in euphoria.

"I really enjoyed your company, Clayton." I told him, after he pulled up in front of his apartment building.

"I really enjoyed spending time with you too, Ruby. We'll have to do it again soon!"

I paused as he prepared to get out the car. "Hey, Clayton," I said, stopping him just as he opened the door. "I know that you said that you don't have any groceries." I reached in my purse and pulled out three twenties. "Here's a few dollars so that you won't have to go hungry."

Clayton looked at the money in my hand and said, "You don't have to do that. I mean, you've already paid for the dinner." But just as quickly as those words left his mouth, he reached over and took the money out of my hand. "Thank you! We definitely have to see each other again soon."

I watched him exit the car and go into his apartment. Although the date was far from perfect, I still believed that he was the man that God had for me.

CHAPTER FIVE

    My life seemed to become more and more complicated as I put forth all of my efforts to get to know Clayton. I was already working quite a few hours at the salon to be able to adequately take care of my son. Apart from my normal obligations, my expenses had increased trying to maintain a long distance relationship with Clayton. I was buying calling cards just about every other day, so that we could talk to avoid running up my cell phone bill. At that time, long distance calls weren't included in most cell phone plans.

    Since Clayton still didn't have a car, I was running back and forth from Springfield to Connecticut so that we could see one another. And since Clayton had already explained that he was trying to get back on his feet, I never asked him for any gas money. I would not dare expect him to pay for our dates either. Though, he never offered. I didn't want to put any pressure on him financially that could possibly tempt him to revert back to his old lifestyle of selling drugs.

    When Clayton decided to start coming to church every Sunday, I had to wake up extra early to get my son and me ready, so that we could take the long drive to pick him up, and still make it back to service on time. It was fine with me, though. I was twenty-one, full of life and energy. Besides that, I was making good money because I had a large clientele, so I didn't mind helping out. I was doing what it took to help save a man's life that I knew had so much potential.

I asked myself at times, "What would Jesus do?" I was also doing what I thought it took to get a husband. I did not want to be the single lady in church that grew old and had never been married. So I made a lot of sacrifices. I did whatever it took because I believed that one day, God would make everything right, and Clayton and I would reflect back on our lives from our rocking chairs and praise God from where He'd brought us from.

Looking back at the younger Ruby, with the more experienced eyes of today, I would have told her, "Stop, you are doing entirely too much! A relationship is supposed to be a reciprocal of giving love and getting the same or more in return than what you have put in." I would even go as far as to say, "Anything you invest in you always expect to get more on your return than what you have put in."

Bishop TD Jakes said in one of his sermons "A man's love has to be sacrificial-*as Christ loved the church and gave Himself...*" A man that gives nothing of himself, is in love with himself, and not with his woman. Why do we as women, accept the crumbs that men throw out to us? Some men only deal with us when it is convenient for them, as they cram us into their *"Things to Do List."* That is why we will go out of our way, and inconvenience ourselves to maintain a lopsided relationship that will leave us broke, broken, and brokenhearted. It leaves us broke, because it completely depletes or strips us of our self-esteem and self-worth, or in some cases financially strained. It leaves us broken- fractured, damaged, no longer in one piece or in working order. Some of us believe that we are incomplete unless we have a man to make us whole. We misconstrue the concept of being taken from Adam's rib, as if we're only a piece to fit into the puzzle of man's wholeness, making us incomplete without them.

The truth is, men are really incomplete without us. God took one whole rib out of Adam, and stood her outside of an incomplete man, and created a whole woman. We become broken mentally, trying to figure out how we could give someone the essence of all that we are, and it's not reciprocated. We become emotionally broken by the pressure of trying to hold a relationship together by ourselves. When we finally decide to let go of it, or the man decides to walk away from us, we're left there holding fragments of our broken heart, trying to figure out how to piece it back together again. I truly believe that the ultimate betrayal in a failed relationship, is not the betrayal that comes from the man's dishonesty to the woman, by him lying, cheating, or straight up using her. It comes from the betrayal of the woman not being completely honest with herself. When she continues to ignore that inner discomfort, when she is doing entirely too much for a man, and it's not reciprocated.

I was trying to be totally empathetic to Clayton's past, to be able to deal with his nasty disposition. However, Clayton seemed to have a sense of entitlement as if I *had* to do the things I was doing for him. He was ungrateful for all that I did to make our relationship work. I was often criticized and fussed at for all the things that he felt I wasn't doing right. He continued to gripe and complain when I was late picking him up from his job, coming from another state. He knew just how much I loved him and wanted to make things work. He knew that I was dating him with a purpose. We both knew that we were dating with the intentions to get married. It was as though I was constantly trying to prove my love to him, to show him that I was worthy of him choosing me to be his wife. It should have been the other way around. However, in spite of all his negativity, Clayton still decided to choose me after all.

CHAPTER SIX

The memory of my engagement was an emotional rollercoaster, just like our courtship. It was the fourth of July in 2001. It was a beautifully bright, sunny and hot day. We had been dating about nine months, and I hadn't seen much of a change in his finances. He still didn't have a car, so I headed out to Hartford to pick up Clayton, because his parents were having a fourth of July gathering at their house. (I was so happy when his parents helped him get a car a few months later).

After we had finished eating at the family gathering, Clayton told me that he was very upset with me and needed to end our relationship. My heart dropped as I quietly tried to talk to him while still in his parent's house.

"What did I do?" I tried hard to fight back the tears.

He told me with a look of displeasure, "I'll tell you when we get in the car."

Totally confused and heartbroken, I hurried to the car before my eyes began to let the tears escape. Once we had gotten into the car, I said, "What on earth did I do to cause you to want to break up with me?"

Clayton said, "Don't act like you don't know what you did. You were talking about me negatively to a client in your styling chair, while my cousin was under the dyer and overheard the whole conversation. She told me everything you said."

My emotions went from sad to angry because I knew that I had never talked about him in a negative light to anybody. Not even my own family. Furthermore, I never discussed anybody's personal business in the salon. I did not want to be labeled as the typical hairstylist that broadcasted everyone's business that sat in my chair.

"Let's call your cousin right now to straighten this out, because I don't appreciate being lied on."

Clayton pulled on my emotions even further and said, "No, it's already done, it's over. I told you from the beginning that I have to be able to trust you not to talk about me or my business to others. You have failed me like everybody else has. I thought that I could trust you."

By this time, the tears were flowing down my face and I said, "You can trust me. This is far from the truth. I told you that I would never betray you. You need to call your cousin right now!"

Clayton kept driving, shaking his head saying, "You know what you did and it's over."

He turned into an unkempt and abandoned lot just before we hit I91 to take him back home. The lot wasn't paved. There was not one beautiful flower in sight. Just sun-torched grass and weeds that were so long that they bent and swept over the dirt spots where the grass was missing.

"Let's get out of the car so we can talk," he said.

The loudness of the cars that zoomed by just before they entered the highway made it very difficult to have any kind of discussion. As we began to walk down a little further there was a homeless man that was quite festive. He wore an American flag t-shirt with matching shorts, wrapped in aluminium foil like garland is wrapped around a Christmas tree. To top it off, he wore a hat made out of aluminium foil, too.

Clayton began to laugh hysterically after the man passed, but I did not see a thing funny. I wanted to know what else he possibly had to talk to me about after telling me our relationship was over.

After he wiped the last smile off his face from laughing profusely, he took me by the hand and said, "This is what you did to me."

Clayton pulled an engagement ring box out of his pocket and opened it in front of me. I was in a state of shock and confusion. I didn't know whether to laugh, cry, or scream. There was then a sigh of relief when I realized that Clayton wasn't going to break up with me after all, but he wanted to spend the rest of his life with me.

I was overcome with joy and tears began to fall from my eyes. My prayers had been answered. Clayton and I embraced and we kissed one another on the cheek.

Clayton had showed little to no affection toward me during our courtship and engagement. I had the hots for him, and although I never had intentions of having sex before marriage, I wanted to at least feel that he was just as attracted to me, as I was to him. I wanted him to attempt to kiss me passionately and caress me so that I could fight hard to resist the urge to give in. Clayton said that he wanted to honor my vow of celibacy, and wanted our marriage to be blessed and not cursed by engaging in premarital-sex. He never tried to tempt me at all in that way. I thought, *He must be the perfect gentleman - almost too perfect.* I wanted to be able to tell Clayton at least a couple of times throughout our year-an-a-half engagement, "Honey, I want you, too, but we have to wait until the wedding night."

Although we were both trying to live a holy and sanctified lifestyle, I still wanted to feel as though I was irresistible, that he was so attracted to me and couldn't keep his hands off of me. However, that was far from the case. From the time we went on our first date, until the time we had gotten married, it was a total of two years with little to no affection. We only kissed one time prior to getting married and I was the one that initiated it.

We sat in the car after a late night date. I looked into his deep brown eyes, as he looked into mine. I waited for him to make the first move and come in closer so that our lips would connect. I waited, but I could no longer resist. My lips magnetically touched his. I had to taste his soft moist and thick flesh. So I opened my mouth and before I knew it, we were kissing passionately for the first time. I wanted to feel what I was about to be working with until death do us part. So I let my hand slip to his lower extremities. With my hands full, I knew he was fully equipped to get the job done. I climbed over the armrest, and onto the driver's side of the car, where I mounted him as I kissed his lips and grinded him, fully clothed. He kissed and sucked my neck softly as I was sitting on top of him. His lips inched lower and lower. His face was right at the entrance of my bosom. I could no longer take it, and pulled my blouse down, along with my bra. Like trying to feed a baby for the first time, he finally latched on. Totally aroused, I began to slowly wind my hips around and around, and up and down. Then faster and faster, I moved them. All of a sudden the brakes were pumped, but not by me.

"We have to wait to the wedding, if we do this now, you would be no good for the wedding," he said, his voice husky.

I was confused by what he meant about I would be no longer good?

I was so embarrassed. I was supposed to be the one to have stopped Clayton from trying to make love to me. Little did I know at the time that this would be the first of many rejections of intimacy that Clayton would give me throughout our seven-year marriage. I had no clue that Clayton would use this one incident of me wanting him prior to our marriage, along with the fact that I had my son out of wedlock against me to accuse me of having a problem in my flesh. Which was crazy since I was celibate for four years before I married Clayton.

The wedding day finally arrived. I went into one of the bedrooms to get dressed. My mother and mother-in-law assisted me and held the gown open for me to step into the dress, so that I would avoid smudging my make-up trying to pull it over my head. It was the most beautiful Victorian styled wedding gown. The collar was high, without it looking overly exaggerated. The neckline of the dress dropped and traced my young cleavage just enough to arouse the imagination. The gown hugged my small waistline to perfection. The front of the A-lined shaped dress slightly kissed the floor, while the long train on the back thoroughly caressed it. As I walked into the living room I was greeted by my five-year-old son, whose face lit up with excitement as he said, "Mommy, you look like a Barbie doll."

I hugged him and gave him a kiss, then we proceeded to

take the pre-wedding photos.

The wedding was at Clayton's uncle's church, because our church was entirely too small to accommodate our guest list. As the long stretch white limousine slowly cruised up State Street, less than a mile before the church, butterflies began to invade my stomach, as the reality of what was about to take place finally began to sink in. I was about to marry the man of my dreams, the answer to my prayers, regardless of how far he was from being perfect.

We finally arrived at the beautiful white church, with the steeple on the top. My heart was beating so hard that I could feel the vibration of the rhinestone necklace I wore pulsating as if it had a heartbeat.

I went into the first lady's office, which had been turned into a temporary bridal chamber for me, and waited for my special moment to walk down the aisle of the church. It was the moment that I had dreamed of, to be chosen by someone to share the rest of my life with. When all eyes were on me, and the groom could stick his chest out proudly at his choice, as I walked gracefully to meet him at the altar.

I waited with great anticipation until finally, the first lady walked in and said, "It's time."

I slipped on my glass slippers and stood up and walked out of the office and faced the double French doors of the sanctuary. When the double doors were opened, I could hear the whispering yelps and babbles of the guests, as they expressed their adoration. The organist played "Here comes the bride," as I slowly made my way to the front of the church. Tears began to roll down Clayton's face as his eyes were fastened on me.

Once I stood before Clayton, I pulled out my white

handkerchief bordered in lace to wipe the beads of sweat from his forehead, and tears from his face.

The crowd responded with "awws" just as a soundtrack of music with a soft and lovely melody began to play. The minister handed Clayton the microphone and he began to sing.

It was a melody I never heard before. A Clayton original melody! My prince had composed a song to tailor fit me, his princess.

"On this special day I dedicate my life to you, when no one else was around you were there... I want to tell the world that you've been good to me... for God sent me an angel like you to rescue me out of my hurt and shame..."

All of a sudden Clayton dropped to his knees in the middle of the song and continued to sing,

"...and I'll get down on my knees and tell the world how much you mean to me...honey, I love you today. Honey, I love you today."

Tears and sweat began to run down Clayton's face as he sang with all of his heart and soul. I pulled out my lace handkerchief once again to reach down to dab the tears from my eyes, and to wipe the sweat and tears from Clayton's face. I extended my hand to help him back to his feet.

After we exchanged vows, Clayton and I went in for our kiss. It wasn't a smooth kiss at all. To make it even more awkward, it was a lengthy and bumpy kiss, as if we were trying to convince the crowd that we knew what we were doing.

The reception was a sit down dinner because dancing and drinking were not allowed at a sanctified, Pentecostal wedding. However, I was able to greet all of my guests and take pictures with them.

The reception soon came to a close, and it was time for my husband and me to go home to our apartment and finally consummate our marriage. We brought all of our wedding gifts and cards in and Clayton decided that we should open all of the gifts right then. I really wasn't thinking about opening wedding gifts at the time. I was anxious for Clayton to unwrap me, his ultimate gift, but I played along with him as if I was excited to open every last one of our wedding gifts.

We finally came down to the last gift. I could feel my temperature rising and my nerves getting jittery as I anticipated our first night together. Clayton had gotten up, and removed the last gift from his lap, and walked past me. He grabbed the box with all of our cards from the wedding and opened each card and read every last one on them, placing the money to the side. He counted all of the money and began talking about how the money would help us pay the rent that was due soon.

I began to yawn and laid my head on the armrest of the couch, as to give him the hint that I was exhausted, and we needed to get the honeymoon started sooner rather than later. After that didn't seem to get his attention, I got up and took a shower, and oiled and perfumed my body down. I was hot and nervous all at the same time, but my sweet aroma filled the bedroom as I slipped on my white sheer and lace negligee.

I laid there with great anticipation of my husband making sweet love to me for the very first time. I fell asleep briefly waiting for him to finish taking his long shower.

"Ruby," I heard Clayton calling me as he gave me a gentle nudge. The smell of his cologne intoxicated me, and we started kissing passionately. Clayton was fully awake in every way. He kissed my neck and made a trail down to my breasts. He worked his way down to my lower parts. I suddenly felt shy and tried to resist. I closed my legs and wiggled my bottom, while pushing his face away. But Clayton had me submit to him without saying a word as his lips and tongue were doing the talking. I obeyed and relaxed as I clutched the back of his head in total ecstasy. I had underestimated Clayton, he had way more experience than what I thought.

Clayton had eaten the appetizers until he was full, and now he was ready for the main course. He stopped and put on a condom and said, "We're not ready for a baby."

"But I'm on birth control. You know that."

I had started taking birth control pills at least three months prior to the wedding.

"We can never be too sure. We are not in the position to have any slip-ups."

I nodded in agreement. Clayton pulled me into him to caress my back and beyond, as I laid on top of him. He rolled over and hovered over me as he tried to make his way in. Clayton was well endowed so it took time for him to enter in. It had been four years since I was intimate with anyone. However, once he gained access, he kept at it until my cup overflowed.

Clayton picked me up out of the bed, and carried me into the living room. He gently laid me on the floor, where he drove into me nonstop until my insides began to quake. My love again rushed out, like an ever flowing river.

CHAPTER SEVEN

The sound of a motor from a boat rumbled in the distance. The waves began to crash up against the car, as movement from the rescue boat pushed the water forward.

"Hey...over here...Help us, please!"

My son and I waved our hands frantically while hollering out, as the rescue boat made its way toward us. The heavens became an open floodgate and rain continued to pour out of the sky with no indication that it was ever going to stop. The boat slowed and inched its way slowly toward the car.

Two men wearing lifejackets yelled out to us. "Keep calm. We're trying to get to you." The motor quieted as they turned it off to make the boat as steady as possible. One of the men jumped out of the boat to push it up against the car, so that it could be an easy transition for us. The man that remained on the boat reached out to me.

"Take my hand," he yelled.

"No, get my son first," I cried.

My son may have appeared to them to be a full grown man, but he was still my 20-year-old baby. I wanted to make sure that he was out of harm's way first.

"Mom, I want you to go," my son said.

I turned to him. "Listen to me. Go! I'll be right behind

you."

Reluctantly, my son heeded my command and grabbed the stranger's hand. The man gave my son a lifejacket because the water was very choppy and worst-case scenario, if the boat had flipped over, we'd have a fighting chance to survive.

Once he secured my son in the boat, the man extended his hand once again, to pull me into the boat. Too afraid that if I reached out too far, I would slip and go plunging face first into the murky waters. I hollered, "I can't go. I can't swim."

"Yes, you can. Come on. You can trust me! Take my hand."

The last time I trusted and taken a man's hand, it turned into one of the biggest disasters of my life.

It was only two months after my marriage to Clayton and the intimacy completely stopped. I thought that our wedding night was an indication that Clayton would have no problem loving me. I began to feel our wedding night was only an initiation, performance, or bait, to have me wrapped around his fingers. Besides that, Clayton knew that all of my sisters and friends would ask me how it was, since there was no intimacy prior to our wedding night.

After the wedding night, Clayton found any and everything to argue and criticize me about. I was trying to be the best wife that I could possibly be, but it seemed like the more energy that I exerted trying to make Clayton happy, the more miserable he became. For example, a week after we had gotten married, I came home and Clayton wasn't talking to me. He walked around with a nasty attitude as I hurried to finish dinner. I tried asking him what was wrong and he continued to ignore me. I tried to hug him and kiss him and he pushed me away. My feelings were crushed as I racked my brain trying to figure out what I had done wrong. I had awakened extra early that morning and made breakfast for Clayton before he went to work. I also ironed his clothes, and started preparation for dinner, before I rushed to get to work. So I couldn't figure out what I'd done to make him angry.

After I finished dinner and fixed our plates, I sat down at the table to eat my food. Although, I didn't have much of an appetite with Clayton not talking to me.

"Did you have a good day at school?" I asked my son, trying to break the uncomfortable silence in the room.

"Yes, Mom," he answered.

That had been the only interaction at the table that night. I got my son settled in bed, then took a long bath and put on my red sexy negligee, hoping that would put Clayton in a better mood. *Maybe he was stressed from being on his feet all day selling shoes,* I thought.

I went into our bedroom and saw Clayton laying with his hands behind his head, staring at the ceiling in deep thought. I climbed into the bed and laid my head on his chest. I nestled my forehead and nose underneath his neck and chin. Then, I moved on top of him and kissed his lips. Clayton lifted me off him and slid me over to the side.

"I'm not in the mood for that." He turned on his side, with his back facing me, and reached on the nightstand to turn off the lights. And then he went to sleep.

I cried myself to sleep that night as the feeling of rejection pierced through my heart like a razor sharp sword. The next morning, I got out of bed broken-hearted. I went into the living room to pray before Clayton woke up, and before I started breakfast.

I was in the kitchen cooking when my husband finally

walked in.

"Do you know what upset me yesterday?" he asked.

I said, "No, Honey. I asked what was wrong with you, but you didn't tell me. I racked my brain trying to figure out what it was. I-"

Clayton cut me off. "You forgot to make the bed! I had to come home from work and make the bed."

I said, "I'm sorry, Clayton, I was so busy trying to make breakfast, and iron clothes, and get Ty ready for school, and prep the dinner so that it could be ready shortly after you got home from work."

Clayton held his hand up to stop me. "There are no excuses for nastiness. I refuse to live in a nasty house. My mother trained me from the second my feet hit the floor to make the bed. Now I don't know what kind of home training you've had, but I'm not going to tolerate this."

Clayton questioned and criticized not only my ability to be a wife, but also to be a woman. Housekeeping should be a part of a woman's DNA, he often told me. I kept the whole house practically spotless. I was trying with all of my might to be the perfect wife and I failed at the simplest task. He overlooked all of the things that I did right, how I worked tirelessly to make sure that he was taken care of. It was only our first week of marriage and I felt as though I was trying earnestly to win my husband's love. I just wanted to make Clayton happy, but my efforts seemed to be failing, as he seemed to grow more and more miserable every day.

Clayton would come home about two or three in the morning just about every night. He claimed it was because he was having a hard time adjusting to life in Springfield, Massachusetts. He just couldn't seem to cut his ties with his connections in Hartford. He said that he had to drive back there, to get away, clear his mind, and visit his old friends.

I told him that I would love to meet some of his friends and he didn't have to go alone all of the time. He told me that he needed that time by himself to think, and besides that, most of his friends would not understand me because I was into the church, and they weren't. There was one friend in particular named Reggie that he claimed was like a brother to him. That's why it puzzled me when he didn't attend our wedding.

"See, you think that when I come in late, I'm out running the streets and up to no good. I would have you to know, that I was out doing the Lord's work," Clayton told me one night. "Reggie received the Holy Ghost. He is now saved. I was praying all night with Reggie, he started speaking in tongues and shaking and praising God."

"Well, with Reggie's new conversion to Christ, it shouldn't be a problem with me accompanying you to visit him and his family in Hartford. He should be able to understand me now," I said.

Clayton didn't say a word, and turned his back to me as he always did, and went to sleep.

CHAPTER EIGHT

I had plenty of restless and sleepless nights. Six months had passed since Clayton had touched me. I would often get out of bed in the middle of the night and go into the living room, and fall on my knees to pray, or even sometimes to lay out in the middle of the floor of our bedroom to silently cry out to God. I was hoping that somehow He would answer me and give me some relief. Or better yet, that He would allow my husband to desire to love me and make love to me once again.

I was beginning to think that something was wrong with me, that it was my fault that my husband did not want to show me any type of affection. I knew that I had my son prior to knowing Clayton. I thought he was turned off by my imperfections. *Maybe the few stretch-marks that I had due to carrying my son was a direct turn-off to him*, I often thought. I began to feel so unattractive, so I decided that we needed to have a real discussion on why we were not intimate. I prepared myself for bed as I always did, hoping that my body oils, lotions, and seductive perfume would somehow hypnotize him, and he'd desire to make passionate love to me. I got into bed that night, and it was the same torturing treatment that my husband gave me every night. He'd turn over with his back facing me, tuck both his hands between his legs, and lay into a fetal position before going to sleep.

This particular night, I was at my wits' end and was not about to let it go down as it usually did. I needed to resolve this problem. Maybe if he told me what I was doing wrong, I could have worked on whatever it was.

I nudged him. "Honey, Honey...wake up."

He played possum for a few minutes, but I continued to tap on his shoulder-blade until I got a response from him.

He turned over, not bothering to hide his aggravation. "Ruby, what do you want? I'm tired."

"We need to talk."

He said, "What is it now, Ruby?"

I wanted to say, I'll tell you "*what it is now* and *what it has been*" for the past eight months of my life being married to you. My life has been flipped upside down and turned inside out, until I am unsure of who I am and why I chose to love someone who makes it almost impossible to love. I hate the fact that I have been paying all of the bills, while you cry and complain about how little money you're making selling women's shoes. You need to man up, and take whatever you're making to contribute to our household, and stop using how little you make as an excuse not to put forth any effort to contribute at all. If you're so unhappy about how little you make and your inability to support your family, then work a second or third job to do whatever it takes as a man to be the provider for your family.

I wanted to say all of that. But I chose the more loving approach.

"Ruby I don't have all night," Clayton said. "I have to go to work tomorrow. What do you want to talk about?"

I was trying to figure out how I was going to start the conversation because Clayton would always get so easily offended. He often took my words and twisted them to mean something totally opposite of what I wanted to say to him. I was always trying to explain and defend myself to Clayton. I knew that I had to choose my words very wisely if I wanted to get the issues resolved in our marriage. I had put off the conversation long enough. The last time that we tried to discuss our intimacy issue, Clayton didn't talk to me for two-and-a-half weeks. So I avoided it, thinking it would correct itself.

Clayton seemed to be totally unbothered by the fact that we had a sexless marriage at a time when we should have still been honeymooning.

"Clayton, you know that I love you. I desire so much to be with you."

Clayton interjected, "You're with me now."

I replied, "Come on, Clayton, you know what I mean. I want to be intimate with you, my husband. It has been six months since we've made love...I miss you."

Clayton said, "Oh, here we go again" as he threw the covers off of him, got out of the bed, and took off his pajamas.

"What are you doing?"

He answered, "I'm about to get some fresh air."

"Clayton, please don't do this. Don't leave. All I wanted was to see if there was something that I could work on to make you desire to be with me again. My body's craving your love..."

Clayton pulled his jeans up and said, "Just because you have a problem in your flesh and can't control your sexual urges, you're not about to put the blame on me!"

He snatched one of his folded, long sleeved cotton shirts out of the dresser drawer, and quickly jerked it over his head. He continued to shred me into pieces with his tongue. "You've been dealing with this long before I met you. You're the one that had a child at seventeen. Oh yeah, and I had to stop you from sleeping with me before our wedding day."

"Clayton, I can't believe you're throwing this up in my face." I started crying hysterically, but he showed me no mercy.

Clayton put his navy blue suede jacket on and further drove the dagger into my heart when he said, "Yeah, and I remember what you told me happened between you and your father."

I could not believe my ears. Clayton was using what I had told him in confidence about the abuse that my sisters and I suffered as children. Clayton reached beyond ground level to hurt me. Better yet, he stooped down to the pits of hell to rip every ounce of my heart and soul clean out of my body.

I screamed out in hurt, anger, and utter disbelief. "I can't believe that you would use something that I had no control over in my childhood as a weapon against me, when all I want is your love!"

Clayton ignored my cries as he stormed out of the bedroom and out of our apartment. I collapsed onto the floor of our bedroom, curled up in a fetal position and rocked back and forth as I cried uncontrollably. As the fountain of tears slowly began to dry up from my eyes, I decided to have dialogue with the Lord, hoping to see if He would answer the questions that Clayton would not.

"Lord, why? I know I was taught not to question you, but I just

don't understand." I sniffled while taking a deep breath, in an attempt to stop more tears from falling. I continued to pour out my heart to God, hoping that He would give me an answer or at least remove the discomforting hurt of my pain-stricken soul. I continued, *"Lord, I thought that You said that Clayton was my husband...the one that You had chosen for me. I'm beginning to second guess if You really spoke to me in the first place. Was I just supposed to pray for his soul to be saved? Did I let my desire of wanting a husband cloud my ability to hear from You clearly? Is there a code of conduct for intercessors as there is for physicians that prohibits them from being romantically involved with their client/patients? Lord, I already knew that Clayton had issues, prior to me saying I do to him. I just thought with Your help, we could plow through them and get them resolved. And I know that You're still able to turn this around. But Lord, what I'm dealing with seems unbearable. It just seems like the more I pray and cry out to You about my marriage the worse he gets. It's like he despises me...like he can't stand to be in my presence. Lord, I will continue to cry out to You. Even though You slay me, yet will I trust You. I will continue to plead my case before You."*

Before I knew it, I was fast asleep on the floor in the same position that I cried out to God in. I was awakened by my husband's voice and a gentle shake on my shoulder, "Honey, come on. Get up off the floor and into the bed. You're going to be sore, and soon you're going to have to get up and go to work."

I squinted, trying to get my bearings. "What time is it, Clayton?"

"It's 4:30am."

I said, "Clayton, where were you?"

"I was out thinking about why our marriage has been in such a disarray, and why there's been no intimacy. So I left to go to a quiet place to pray. And the Lord began to speak to me..." I got up immediately off the floor and sat at the edge of the bed as the tiredness left me instantly. *Perhaps God had decided to give the answer to Clayton because his role as a husband was to lead his family. I guessed that's why He didn't give me the answer*, I thought.

I waited with great anticipation to hear what God had spoken to Clayton, four hours ago when he left the house. Clayton took off his jacket and sat next to me at the edge of the bed and placed it to the side of him. He turned to me, looked straight into my eyes and said, "God is not pleased with us." He paused for a moment, then took a deep breath to gather his thoughts.

"What do you mean He's not pleased with us? We're trying. Well, I can only speak for myself. I'm trying with everything in me that I know to please God. Although we all fall short of His glory as humans. How is it that God told you that He's not pleased with me? Furthermore, how does this relate to us not being intimate?"

"I said God is not pleased with *us*. We are one. You see, Honey, there are some things that God wants us to do together, and until we do them, it's going to remain this way."

"Clayton, what exactly are you talking about? What does God want us to do that we are not doing right now? And how would it interfere with you desiring to be intimate with me, your wife?"

"I know that it doesn't make sense to you, but it makes perfectly good sense to me. You're not going to understand everything the Lord has to tell me as the leader of this family. And I don't expect you to. But I do expect you to trust me as your husband and the leader of this family. You said that God spoke to you and told you that I was your husband, even before I was fully aware of it. I was out on the street doing my own thing and having a good time. Didn't you tell me that you knew that God put us together?"

"Yes, or I would not have married you."

"Okay then, you'll have to trust when I say as your husband, that God has spoken to me. I was trying to figure out what was wrong with me, that caused me not to want to be intimate with you. I mean look at you...you're absolutely beautiful. So I left a while ago to get some answers from God. And God began to speak to me."

The tears began to roll from Clayton's eyes. I was ready and willing to do whatever the Lord wanted us to do to fix it.

"The Lord wants us to do ministry together. When my mother first mentioned you to me, she told me that you were gifted. She said that you were an excellent speaker. She also said that you have a prophetic anointing on your life. Think about it, you spoke me into existence in your life. Then, when I heard you speak for myself for the first time, I was blown away. The Lord told me that you're not utilizing your gift that He has given you to prophesy to people, and until you do, there will be no intimacy."

Of course, his logic didn't make any sense to me. I had already known that I had a calling on my life to minister the word of God to the hurting and lost. I was already bringing the Word when I was called on to do so occasionally. I was constantly studying the word of God, in preparation for what I knew God was calling me to do. So, why would God allow me to have a loveless marriage, in an attempt to provoke me to prepare myself for what I was already trying to continuously prepare myself for. It just didn't make any sense to me. I was not the type of person that was so caught up in titles and positions, that I would walk around labeling myself.

I was a firm believer that whatever gifts that God placed in me "will make room for me" one day. However, I would not dispute what Clayton believed God told him concerning the ice cold issues of intimacy in our marriage.

Maybe it was Clayton who wasn't doing what God wanted him to do. "Honey, what is it that you feel that you're supposed to be doing for God that you are not doing?"

"I know that I'm supposed to be making music...a gospel CD. I wanted to use my talent to sing and write music for the Lord. I could have already made it as a secular artist, but I'd always felt that my talent needed to be used for the church."

"Clayton, that's wonderful. I always believed that you have a gift to sing which could minister to so many people."

"There's a studio in Hartford that I want to use. A friend of mine said that he would give me sessions at a discounted rate. Although it's still not going to be cheap, so every little bit taken off the price will help out somewhat. It's going to take a lot of hours and a lot of money to complete an entire CD. I need your full support and understanding. I know how you get all upset when I come in late. I have to commit a great deal of time to get it done. It doesn't make me feel good as a man, that you're paying all of the bills. I know that once I complete this CD, it will generate so much revenue, that it will significantly change our lives for the better. I'll be able to purchase a salon for you, and you could choose to work at your own leisure. I could finally stop working on commission. I'm tired of selling women shoes. I sell other people's items, and I'm only getting a small percentage of commission in comparison to what they make off of it. I want to sell my own CDs, something that I produced myself. I can't do this by myself. I need your *full* support. Are you with me?"

I thought about it momentarily. I knew Clayton had so much potential. I didn't mind investing in something that I knew could help him, as well as others, come closer to Christ. I just wanted Clayton to be happy. And if him making gospel music could have possibly made him a better person as well as a better husband, it was well worth giving him my full support. The way Clayton was talking, he could be the loving husband and provider that I had envisioned him to be. Most importantly, I was looking at the overall and long-term picture. What was losing money in comparison to losing my marriage?

"Yes, Clayton. You have my full support," I said.

Clayton kissed me on my lips. "That's why I love you, Honey."

"All right, Clayton, when are you planning to start in the studio, so that I can begin to put extra money aside outside of our monthly bills?"

"As soon as you can come up with the money, I will get started."

"Let's wait until Saturday to see how I do at the salon this week."

"Sounds like a plan. I can let him know that I'll be starting on Monday."

Monday was really my only day off, considering that on Sundays we spent most of the day at church. I wasn't happy that he wanted to start his studio sessions on my only day off. I wanted to spend time with him. However, if this was going to be the start of the process to bettering our marriage from what Clayton said, I would just have to bite my tongue and go with the flow of things.

I was exhausted trying to stay awake at work and trying to hide my distress from my co-workers. The cruel things that Clayton said to me the night before consumed my mind. Although we talked, he never apologized for the devastating words that he had spoken to me. If God really had spoken to him, why didn't God tell him to apologize for the cruel things he said to me and for the way that he treated me on a daily basis? Better yet, if he had a human conscience, never mind a God conscience, he would have acknowledged that the things he said to me before he stormed out of the house, were dead wrong.

After I finished curling my client's hair, I went into the bathroom to rub some cold water on my face to help me fully wake up. As I looked at myself in the mirror, the image that stared back at me became extremely blurry and distorted. It was almost impossible for me to see myself, or even know the woman who stared back at me. And just like windshield wipers work hard to wipe the rain away during a torrential downpour to no avail, the more I wiped the tears from my eyes, the harder they fell, and never seemed to end.

Someone knocked on the door, then a voice said, "Come on, Ruby, it's Claudine. Are you still in there? I have to use the bathroom. I've waited long enough."

I quickly shut off the waterfall of tears to try to adjust my voice, so that Claudine couldn't hear the sorrow in my voice, "Okay, I'll be out in a minute."

"Are you okay in there?"

"Yes. I just don't feel too good today. My stomach is a little upset."

Claudine replied, "You're not pregnant, are you?"

"No, Claudine. I'm just not feeling well today, but I'll be out in a few seconds!"

"Well, hurry up since I know that you're all right. I have to use the bathroom. You know that I have a weak bladder!"

I quickly smoothed my hair down, and patted the last bit of moisture off my eyes. I opened the door and Claudine stood right in the doorway and said, "Girl, you don't look well at all. You better get yourself together." She quickly brushed past me to make it into the restroom.

Claudine was the owner of the salon that I worked at called Platinum Finesse Beauty Palace. She was sixty-two years old and had been doing hair for over forty years. Although she was an older hair stylist, she had a large clientele base of all ages. Claudine would work from 6:30am, until almost midnight every night. I remember when I first started working with her, I said I would never work that hard. I am eating my words until this day.

I had to try to pull myself together because we had bible study that night, and I did not want the saints to see that anything was wrong with me.

Only my son and I attended bible study that night, because Clayton had to work. On bible study nights, we always had a short devotional service before our lesson started, in which anyone in the congregation could lead a song. Since there were only a few members that would attend each week, I usually was the one that always led the congregation in a song of praise. I just didn't have a song of praise in my heart anymore. It was a struggle even to sing along with the congregation, but I forced myself to sing anyway.

After bible study was over, Clayton's sister came up to me

and said, "Are you okay? You just don't seem like yourself anymore. You used to be on fire for God when you led the praise and worship service, and I miss watching you do it."

Before I knew it, the tears began to flow out like a river. "I'm okay. But I'm not feeling well today."

"I hope that you're feeling better soon."

"Thanks," I told her and retreated into the restroom. I tried my hardest to pull myself together before I reentered into the sanctuary, but my red eyes told everyone who looked in my face what was really going on. All of the members had already left, with the exception of the pastor and the first lady, because they were still putting things away so that they could close up the church.

Clayton's mother asked me, "Sister Ruby, are you all right? You don't look so good tonight."

I sat next to her where she usually sat in the front of the church, and the tears began to pour out and would not stop. She reached over on the table that was next to her designated first lady's chair, and handed me a few tissues to wipe my eyes.

"Oh sister Ruby, what's going on?"

I continued to wipe the tears from my face, and shake my head, trying to figure out where to start. After all, this was Clayton's mother, so I had to choose my words carefully. However, she was my first lady and spiritual leader even before I knew who Clayton was.

"You know you can talk to me about anything. You're my daughter."

How could I tell my mother-in-law that her son was cruel, mean, not paying the bills, and having problems in the bedroom? I couldn't, so I just told her, "Can you just pray for me? Well, what I mean is, can you pray for us?"

"Is there anything in particular that you need me to pray for?"

"I just need God to fix some things in my marriage."

She replied, "I sense that you're not too comfortable stating in specifics what it is."

"No, not right now."

"Well, I'm going to pray for you right now."

After she had prayed, I felt a little better knowing that she had us covered with her prayers. "Thank you so much. I feel better now," I told her.

She said, "You know I am here for you. You can call me if you need to talk."

"I definitely will. Oh yeah, I'll see you at the hair salon tomorrow."

"Yes, it's time to hook you up again. Good night."

The next day at the salon my mother-in-law was the first client that I had on Thursday.

"You're looking like you're feeling much better today," she told me.

"I do. Thanks again for the prayer last night. It really helped me."

"I do know that prayer still works. You know you can talk to me about anything. We can band together in prayer, and that devil will have to leave you all alone!"

Since my mother-in-law was the only one in the salon at the time, I decided to share what was going on in my marriage. "Okay, I will tell you what's going on. It's kind of hard for me to say it."

I never really felt right addressing my mother-in-law by the title Mother, because my mother was still living. She was a missionary, so that's the name I addressed her with, when I first started going to the church before I married Clayton, and she was okay with that.

"What is it? You know you can trust me."

I said, "All right...Clayton has not touched me for six months..."

She interrupted. "What? Six months?"

I nodded. "It's very painful."

"Well, do you put on your sexy negligee? Like the one's you've gotten from your bridal shower?"

"Yes. I have put on the negligee. I've bought some new ones too, to see if it would change anything."

"And that doesn't work...that doesn't arouse him?" she asked.

"No it doesn't."

"Sister Ruby, I don't know. I don't understand. You are a beautiful young woman, and he's a handsome young man." She continued, "I'm really about to fast and pray to get down to the bottom of this. You all are newly married. You all should be going like rabbits. Just keep on praying, and I know things will get better."

"I will." I felt much better since I let out what was troubling me in my marriage. I didn't talk to my family about my marital issues because I feared they would never forget the turmoil Clayton was taking me through. It felt as though a ton of bricks had been lifted off me, and I had the strength to keep on pressing forward even though it felt as though the tide was pushing against me.

CHAPTER NINE

The current from the flood water was pushing the boat away from the car. There was no more time to waste, so I grabbed the stranger's hand. My son cheered me on, "Come on, Mom. You can do it. It's not that hard."

He pulled me into the boat, and I sighed in relief as I was momentarily out of harm's way. The stranger began to help me put a life jacket on, before they proceeded to restart the motor. Once we were all secure in the boat, we began to sail down our street, which was now a lake.

There was a lady a little farther down the street that waved her hands to be rescued. We slowed to get her. Although we lived on the same street, I had never seen her before. Once she was secure inside of the boat, with her a life jacket on, she seemed to think it was necessary to record a video of us. I was in such a daze or in a state of shock that I waved at her cellphone and smiled as she recorded my son and me. It was a bumpy ride, and I had no clue where the boat was taking us.

I held on tight to the side of the boat that I was on, hoping that it wouldn't flip over with the heavy current. Once we made a right turn onto FM 517, we saw busloads of people on both sides of the road. They had been dropped off by various rescue boats, and were waiting to be taken to a shelter. There was a funeral home to the right of us and a Chevron to the left of us.

"Sorry, folks, the Chevron is as far as we can go," one of our rescuers said. "The National Guard should be here shortly."

I couldn't believe they were just going to leave us out in the elements, as the rain, thunder, and lightning continued to give us a live show. I felt my fury grow with the mayor of Houston as I tried to figure out why he didn't call for a mandatory evacuation. Looking back on it now, so many people would have drowned from being stranded on the roadways, had the mayor called for a mandatory evacuation.

We all continued to wait, many of us still stunned, as there were no government official trucks or boats in sight. Those who rescue people from their flooded homes in the surrounding communities, were brave civilians. In spite of how divided our nation was at the time, with our newly elected president, all of Houston united as one. Civilians risked their own lives in their motor boats and their oversized pick-up trucks to save the lives of their fellow Houstonians. Never once did they stop the progress of our rescue to ask which political party we belonged to. The color of our skin didn't matter either. We were all of the same race that day– the human race. As we waited to be brought to a temporary shelter, more and more people were dropped off. All of us looked as if we had escaped a war zone. Most people clung to their loved ones, in a similar way to how our rain saturated clothing clung to our bodies. Others had trash bags filled with their belongings that they grabbed in haste as they left their flooded homes. There were mothers carrying their newborn babies, wrapped in rain drenched blankets.

As we waited, there was an unusual calm that filled the atmosphere. I guess we all had totally surrendered to the power of nature. It was far too strong for us to continue to fight against it. We were all in survival mode and tried to stay as hopeful as possible. Any negativity displayed would have only made matters worse.

Dogs whimpered as they panted back and forth in front of their owners, as they wondered their fate. All who waited to be rescued wondered what would become of us, as the tormenting sounds of phones sounding off at the same time filled the air. The tornado and flash flood warnings blared as a constant reminder that we were not out of harm's way. The rain continued to beat down on us.

"Lord, would you please let it stop raining, or we'll all perish out here," I prayed. It seemed like the more I prayed, the harder it rained. It was as if the Lord turned deaf ears to my prayers, along with everyone who prayed for the rain to cease. However, this was not the first time when it seemed as if God had closed His ears to my prayers.

I had continued to pray for my marriage, yet nothing changed. I thought that investing in Clayton's passion for music, would make him a happier person. However, the more I seemed to do for Clayton, the more he seemed to despise me. I was handing Clayton hundreds of dollars at a time for studio sessions. It had been a little over six months since he started in the studio and all I'd heard were a couple of demos with instrumental music only. I felt he should have completed at least one single with his vocals on it. He would constantly come in at two and three in the morning, always "coming back from a studio session." He gave me nothing to show for the hours he claimed to have put in at the studio. I was beginning to feel like my money was going elsewhere. I would find lighters in Clayton's pants pockets when I would do his laundry.

"Where did this lighter come from?" I would ask.

"I don't know. That's not mine," he would reply.

That's what he said – each time. I was beginning to think that Clayton thought that I was naïve and stupid, because I held in a lot to keep the peace.

One day while I was cleaning our bedroom, I found a pack of cigarettes, with quite a few still left in the pack. When Clayton came home from work I asked him, "Honey, whose cigarettes are these? They were in our bedroom."

He shrugged. "I don't know where that came from. They are not mine. I must have carried them in off of the bottom of my shoe."

My husband was really going to insult my intelligence with that ludicrous answer.

The thing was, Clayton didn't have to lie and hide things from me. I was his wife. I wanted to know everything about him, his strengths, as well as his weaknesses. I wanted to know the good, the bad, and all of the ugly, so that we could grow stronger and better together as a married couple. But Clayton constantly tried to mask himself from me. It seemed as if he had built this impenetrable brick wall all around himself, and locked me out from getting to the real him. The harder that I tried to penetrate the wall, the thicker it seemed to have gotten, and I was injuring myself in the process.

I recall going to the gas station down the street from our apartment and the store attendant was a young woman that was probably the same age as me.

"Where has your husband been?" she asked.

I replied, "Excuse me?"

"I haven't seen him for a couple of weeks. He usually comes in here and buys his cigarettes and liquor, but I hadn't seen him."

My heart dropped at the realization that another woman knew the type of cigarettes and liquor that my husband liked to purchase and I had no earthly clue. Why did Clayton feel the need to keep on lying to me about who he really was? Could that have been the reason why Clayton despised me, because he felt the need to suppress who he really was from me? Perhaps that's why he stayed away from me so much.

I waited in my car until Clayton came home that night. My son was already inside sound asleep. I wanted to be able to talk to Clayton about what the attendant at the gas station had revealed to me. I could see his car about to turn into our driveway. I watched from the passenger seat of my car, what appeared to be a reddish-orange light glow and flicker off and on inside of Clayton's car. I saw it for myself. It was the light of Clayton's cigarette bud, as he hurried to get the last few puffs in before he made it home to his "overly religious" wife.

Clayton had me all wrong. I would have never turned my nose up at him, as if I was better than him because he smoked and drank liquor. No, I wasn't overly religious at all. I just loved God with all of my heart and soul, and somehow that seemed to intimidate and irritate Clayton.

He pulled up his car right next to mine, unaware of my presence, as I laid back in the passenger's seat, in the front of the car. I wanted there to be no denying that what the attendant at the gas station revealed to me was the truth. I slowly rolled my window down and waved at Clayton. He hesitated before he let his window down. A look of guilt and exhaustion consumed his face. As he started talking through the opened window of his driver's door, I sat in my car with my window fully down waiting for one of his lies to slap me in the face.

"Ruby, why are you waiting out here in your car?"

"I wanted to meet you out here when you came home."

"What is going on that it couldn't wait until I got in the house?"

"I went to the gas station and I had to hear from another woman what kind of cigarettes and liquor you like to buy."

"Ruby, what are you talking a-?"

Before he could finish getting his lie out, I said, "Just stop it. Please don't tell me another lie. I already knew that you smoked. I'm constantly finding lighters in your clothing. Yet you keep on insulting my intelligence by pretending that they just keep on magically appearing in our laundry. Then when I practically found a whole pack of cigarettes in our bedroom, you could have admitted then that they were yours, but you didn't. You still found a way to insult my intelligence. Did you really think that I believed you when you said that you carried them in off of the bottom of your shoe? Now tonight, I will not let you deny this. What hurts the most is not the fact that you smoke or drink. It is the fact that the store attendant knows what kind of cigarettes my husband likes to smoke. She also knows what kind of liquor my husband likes to drink, and I don't. I live with you every day, yet another woman knows you better than me. Put yourself in my shoes for a minute. How would you feel if a stranger, a man, told you something about me that you had no earthly clue about? How would that make you feel as my husband? I hope that you would feel just as foolish and humiliated as I did."

The tears began to roll down my face, as I shook my head in utter disappointment and brokenness. Instead of apologizing, Clayton started going off about how wrong the store attendant was for giving out personal information of customers.

"I could have her lose her job for that."

"Would you stop! You're missing the whole point! She didn't purposely try to expose your habits to me. She naturally assumed that since I was your wife, I knew." I released a frustrated sigh. "Clayton, we should be so close that neither one of us has secrets."

An eerie quietness fell over him and I didn't know how to take it. I was used to him blowing up and driving off, leaving me crying and praying in the house. Clayton's face began to softened and he said,

"You just seem so perfect and holier than thou, that I thought that you would judge me. I tried to stop smoking when we first got together, but whenever I'm stressed it helps to calm my nerves. When I moved back here, a few weeks after we had gotten married, I started back smoking. I didn't want to hide it from you, but I just didn't think that you would understand. I'm not proud of this at all. I'm definitely not happy with the way that you've found out about it. But I'm glad that you know now. I feel like a heavy weight has been lifted off of me."

"Look Clayton, I'm your wife, your helpmate. All you had to do was come to me and let me know you were having a struggle, and we could have prayed together on those matters.

Honey...we're supposed to be one."

At that very moment, Clayton opened the door of his car, got out, reached over and opened my door.

"Come on Ruby, let's go inside."

Clayton took my hand and led me back into our small apartment and into our bedroom. He pulled me into him and looked deep into my eyes. "Honey, I love you," he said.

My heart melted as he pressed his thick and moist lips into mine. His nicotine flavored lips and tongue tasted like sweet milk chocolate to me, as I took every ounce of them in. It had been a little over a year since Clayton had showed me any type of affection. I wasn't going to let the fact that he had lied to me stop Clayton from making love to me.

I moaned as his hands went underneath my shirt and around the small of my back. He slowly began to caress his way up, as we were lost in each other's lips. His fingers stopped at the back of my bra and he fidgeted with it until it finally popped opened. I lifted up my hands to the ceiling to assist him as he took off my shirt and bra. He unzipped the back of my skirt, and it hit the floor, and I was standing before him with only a black thong on. Clayton paused for a moment, and stared at me as if I was a new woman who stood before him. He took me by the hand and led me back to the bed, where he sat down and pulled me in close to him. Our lips connected instantly and Clayton began to softly suck on my bottom lip, then down to my chin. He inched his way down to my neck, then lower and lower he kissed, as I massaged his back and neck. I kissed the top of his head and told him how much I loved him and missed him.

"I miss you too, Ruby." Clayton scooted all the way back

on the bed, bringing his head up to the headboard and onto the pillows. I locked my arms around the back of his neck to prevent myself from falling off. I slipped off Clayton's shirt as I sat on top of him, then slid both my hands over his well-built chest. I slowly worked my fingertips up to the center of his chest and began to gently pull the curly hair that was in the middle of his chest as I massaged, caressed, and kissed it.

I slowly worked my fingers down to trace out his nicely etched stomach. I slid back a little so that I could unbuckle Clayton's belt and pants. I slid them all the way down to his ankles. He kicked them off the rest of the way, as I pulled his boxers down. Clayton pulled me onto his stomach and slid both of his hands underneath my thong as he caressed my buttocks. He allowed both of his thumbs to lock on to my thong and he slid the thong down as I laid there on top of him. I was ready to feel my husband inside of me. I was ready to take him for a ride.

Clayton stopped me and sat up. He reached over to go into his top drawer to get a condom. I should have been used to it. Clayton was determined not to get me pregnant. But after a year of waiting, him putting on a condom was the least of my worries. I just wanted my husband to make love to me. We resumed our positions. I held on to my husband like an experienced bull rider. I didn't know when the next time Clayton was going to decide to make love to me, so I wanted to savor every moment.

I was very hopeful that things were going to change for the better. Especially since Clayton didn't have to hide the fact that he smoked cigarettes and drank alcohol from me any longer. I truly believed that me accepting Clayton for who he really was, would be the start of him opening up to me more and more. I hoped that we would have no more secrets between the two of us and the miracle of marriage would finally take its course—the two of us could finally become one.

CHAPTER TEN

Our winter hair show was quickly approaching. Claudine decided to use a gospel music theme for the show since it was near Christmas. Our salon was hosting the event, but Claudine wanted surrounding salons in Springfield to participate in order to bring unity back into the divided hair industry community.

We all had rehearsed a few months prior to the show actually taking place. Each hair category had a choreographed routine to fit the scene. Claudine had hired a professional choreographer to help us put on a show to remember. Since it was a gospel music themed show, Clayton wanted me to ask Claudine if he could sing one of his gospel songs.

"Girl, we only have three weeks left until our hair show and I'm so excited!" Claudine exclaimed as I walked into the salon to get ready for my first client.

"I know, Claudine, I cannot wait. It's really going to be an awesome hair show. You've been working your butt off to make sure that it goes off just right," I said.

"You've been working just as hard and I'm grateful for your help and support."

"It's no problem at all," I said. "You know I love what I do. There is no better way to express my passion for doing hair than by being a part of this hair show. I really thank you for giving me the opportunity to be a part of something great."

"I'm so glad that you are a part of the Platinum Finesse family," Claudine said. "When you first came to the salon and asked me if you could work here, I was a little hesitant because most young stylists come with a lot of drama. I quickly saw that you were different. You were already established and stable in the industry. I love that you're into the health of the hair. You show up on time to work every day, and put out quality work. And most importantly, you love God and your family. One day I plan on leaving the business to you."

That made me smile. "I'm honored that you trust me enough to take on what you've worked so hard to build over the years. Thank you, Claudine."

"I know good people when I see them. Let me know if there's anything you need."

That caused me to shift, take a deep breath, then I said, "Well, there is one small favor I need to ask of you."

"What is it, Ruby?"

"Um, my husband wanted to know if he could sing one of his gospel songs for the hair show."

The smile left her face, replaced by a nervous expression. "I don't know. There are only three weeks left until the show, and we already have everything timed out just right. He hasn't been to any of the rehearsals. Ruby, can he really sing?"

I giggled and said, "Yes, Claudine, he can really sing."

She nodded. "Well first, I want to hear a demo of what he's going to sing."

"So, is that a yes?" I asked.

"Yes, it is. But I'll need to hear what he'll be singing first. Remember, I am trusting your word, Ruby."

I grabbed Claudine and squeezed her tight. "Thank you. I promise you will not be disappointed!"

"I better not, or that will be your bee-hind." She chuckled. "I already have put a lot into this hair show, and it has to be done in the spirit of excellence."

I reassured her as I went back to work, giddy from the news. I finally would be able to hear at least one of the songs that Clayton was working on in the studio.

That night, when Clayton walked in from work, he had a look of frustration and exhaustion painted all over his face.

"Hey, Honey. How did your day go?"

"It's the same old stuff," he huffed. "I'm just selling women's shoes. I can't wait to get out of this."

Hoping my news would put him in a better mood, I said, "Hey Honey, I asked Claudine today if you could perform in the gospel hair show. She said, even though you hadn't been to any rehearsals, she would let you participate as long as she heard a preview of what you'll be singing."

A smile slowly broke out over Clayton's face. "Oh, that's great news, and especially after the kind of day that I had. Let me get the keyboard and get to practicing." He raced into the bedroom and I felt a moment of dejection. Clayton didn't bother to thank me, kiss me, or even hug me to show his gratitude.

I followed closely behind him. "What are you going to sing?" I asked.

"I want to surprise you guys."

"Honey, maybe you didn't hear me when I told you that Claudine wants to hear a demo of the music that you'll be performing *before* the day of the hair show."

"Ruby, you know I got this. Just tell her that I want it to be a surprise. Just reassure her that I know what I'm doing." Clayton attached his headphones to his Yamaha keyboard to silence the speakers for a private practice session. He put on the headphones, closed his eyes, bobbed his head, and patted one of his feet as if there was a base drum in front of him. His fingers danced up and down the keys of his keyboard, as he moved his lips to the music. There was utter silence in the room as I stood before him, except the sound of the clicking of the keys on the keyboard, and the sound of his foot patting. And I suddenly became invisible, as I stood before him.

The day of the hair show finally arrived. I had practically spent the entire night at the salon preparing my models. I was the youngest hair stylist in our salon, so I wanted all of Springfield to see that Platinum Finesse Beauty Palace, was a salon of hair diversity and versatility. I wanted everyone to see a younger and experienced stylist, working with an older and more seasoned stylist in harmony.

I headed to the salon early since I was one of my own models in the hair extension category. I had installed long and sleek hair extensions on myself, with brown and honey blonde highlights. I razor cut the front of it, so that the shortest layer fell just below my chin. Then from that shortest layer, the rest of the hair angled and followed a perfect slope––from my neck to my collar bone, down to my breast, and then hitting the upper part of my waist. I was in the mirror admiring my own work as I shook my head from side to side to do *the body check test*—making sure that my hair swayed effortlessly. Just then, Claudine walked into the salon with snow all over her hat and boots. I knew the blizzard-like weather had her concerned, but Claudine tried to mask her worries.

"The show must go on," she said. "I've put too much money into this show, and we've sold almost five hundred tickets to people, so we can't let them down."

"Yes, it must go on," I replied. "I know that I'm ready for it. No snow, blizzard, or not even an abominable snowman could stop this show from happening."

Claudine's eyes lit up. "That's right, Ruby. It's going to be fabulous, a hair show to remember!"

"Only you have what it takes to bring all of these salons together. You are so well respected in the community, not only because of your longevity, but you have the ability to service a clientele of all generations. Most older hair stylists are stuck in a time zone of outdated hair styles, but not you. You continue to stay current."

Claudine looked deep into my eyes and said, "Ruby, you know how I continue to stay current? I never stop learning. I learn from everyone I'm around. The moment that I stop learning is when it's time for me to go home to glory, because there will be no more use for me here. The key to having longevity in this business, is that you have to be intergenerational. I want to be able to touch the lives from all ages and from all walks of life." She turned to the mirror. "Now, come over here and help me fix my hair. You have yours looking fabulous, girl!"

"Okay, Mrs. Claudine, I'm about to hook you up."

As I began styling her hair, she said, "By the way, did you get a chance to talk to Shirley?"

Shirley was an older stylist that had worked with Claudine

for years.

"No, the last time that I heard from her was yesterday when she was going to meet Lyn to pick up her outfit for the show."

"Well, Ruby, it's a mess. Lyn didn't show up, and told Shirley that something came up. She's supposed to be meeting Shirley at the hair show to bring her outfit around eleven o'clock this morning. I told Shirley that she needs to bring a back-up outfit, just in case this lady doesn't show up. It seems like something went horribly wrong to me. This woman has been stalling to show Shirley this outfit. Can she really sew?"

"Yes, I'm most certain she can," I said. "My mother-in-law has worked with Lyn for many years. Lyn told her that years ago, she made clothing for Ebony Fashion Fair in New York City."

Claudine looked skeptical. "Well, it's taking her an awfully long time to get it done. I sure hope that you're right. But if you trust your mother-in-law's word, then that's good enough for me."

"Yes, I do trust her word," I said.

"Speaking of trust, I never heard the demo of the music your husband is going to sing today."

"Claudine, he wanted the song to be a surprise for the both of us. I promise that you don't have anything to worry about."

"I know I better not. Now I'm trusting your word." She leaned back and let me finish her hair.

I headed back home, and navigated my way through the snowy roadways. The night before the hair show, my son had spent the night at my sister's house, so that I would be able to give my full attention as I prepared for it. They met me there, later on that day. When I walked into our apartment, Clayton was at his keyboard with his headphones on. He pretended that he was so engrossed in his music that he couldn't acknowledge my presence. Our apartment was very small, so there was no way that he couldn't see me as I walked through the door.

I stood in front of him, and waved my hand into his face to break the trance that he appeared to be in.

"Hello, Honey," I said.

Clayton flinched as he appeared to snap out of his trance.

"Hey." Clayton wiped his hand down his face as if he were exhausted. "What time is it?"

"Almost ten."

"I'm finishing up the last touches on this song. I got up shortly after you left."

"So, how is it coming along?"

"Good. I'm just about finished."

"I'm so excited to finally hear the music that you've been spending so much of your time working on."

"See, you don't understand how much time and money that it takes to make quality music in the studio. I could've already had a CD, but I just didn't want to put anything out there. I'm looking for my music to be up there with the giants of the gospel music industry like Kirk Franklin, Fred Hammond, Yolanda Adams, and Donnie McClurkin. I know it's been a while since you've been investing in my studio time, but you can't rush greatness."

I smiled at his enthusiasm. "Well, I better let you finish up. I can't wait to see you perform your music in front of all of my clients, family and friends. I hope you know, I've been bragging on just how talented you are to all of them. I give you the best of my blessings for your performance this afternoon. Now I need to hurry up and get ready. I have to be at the hotel no later than noon to help set up."

"Thank you, Ruby. I'll see you a little later."

I hurried into the bathtub after wrapping up my hair to prevent it from getting wet. I chose to take a bath over a shower so the steam wouldn't mess up my hair. I slid my closet door open and grabbed both of the outfits I planned to wear, and placed them both on the bed. The first outfit I picked for the first half of the hair show was an all-black outfit. It was a fitted sweater, with fur that wrapped four inches around the top of it, and slightly hung off the shoulders. I slid on my black tights, then stepped into my leather skirt, with a split up the back of it. I put on my leather stiletto boots, that allowed just enough of my calf to peek out of them. They had fancy black fashion buckles on the side of the outer part of the boot. I placed my silver fashion belt around my waist, that accentuated my curves. I wore long, sexy silver earrings that dangled and could be seen through my long hair.

I threw on my leather coat and grabbed some of my belongings, as Clayton help me carry the rest of them to my car. It was a struggle not to fall or drop anything as I walked in the snow in stiletto boots, but I made it to my car without an incident.

I gave myself enough time to get there safely before noon, because of the icy road conditions. By the time I got there Claudine had already set up a room for our salon, so that we could touch-up our models' hair and change our attire when it was time. My second outfit was a beautiful winter white leather and rabbit fur-fitted jacket. The collar and the bottom of the jacket, along with part of the sleeves were leather. However, the front and the back of the jacket was covered in cream and tan rabbit fur. The sleeves were specially designed. The leather part of the sleeve stopped at about three quarter lengths of my arms, and the bottom of the sleeve slightly belled out, and was covered in rabbit fur. They were made to hug my arms with adjustable crisscrossed leather laces on the outside of each sleeve. I wore a lightweight cream shirt underneath the jacket. My skirt was suede, and the color was camel-brown. It had rusted gold zippers that laid on the top of each of my hips. It also had a rusted gold zipper that went from the bottom of the front of the skirt, all the way to the top of my waist. My boots were the same color suede as my skirt, with pieces of winter white leather that encased the top of them. The top of the tongue of the boots were leather and winter white, the rest of it was in camel-brown suede. The shoe laces were like a jigsaw pattern of winter white intermingled with camel-brown. I had planned to make a fashion statement to say the least.

After I finished hanging my outfit in the closet, Shirley gave me a dirty look and didn't speak to me. I brushed it off and continued setting up. Shirley stood there in what appeared to be a throw-on dress. She had an attitude as she struggled to fix her model's hair. It was apparent that Lyn hadn't shown up yet with Shirley's outfit. The tension was so thick in the room that it slowly began to choke out all of our excitement.

The awkward silence was broken by the voice of Claudine.

"I can't take this anymore," she exclaimed. "Ruby, come

and help Shirley fix her model's hair. Can't you see she's having a hard time? She needs your help."

I stopped working on my model and walked over to help Shirley.

"I got it! I don't need any help from you," she snapped. "All I need is for this lady that your mother-in-law referred to me to show up with my outfit! So, you can march your little butt back over there and continue to mind your own business. If my outfit doesn't get here soon, you better keep an eye on that pretty little cream outfit that you have in the closet, because I have a mind to pour something all over it!"

I quickly walked back over to my model and continue to put the final touches on her hair. *Shirley's just simply blowing off steam, she's not a real threat to me...*I thought. Shirley was a sixty-plus year old lady that was provoked to anger, by an unreliable so-called fashion designer.

Shirley's phone suddenly rang, and I could hear her giving the person she was talking to directions to come into our suite. Shirley hung up the phone with a sigh. Then she said with excitement, "She's finally here!" The whole room let out gasps of relief.

Lyn entered our suite with an oversized and bulky trash bag that hung over her arm. Apparently, she was using it as a garment bag. Shirley stepped out of the room to express her displeasure for Lyn coming so late. Lyn apologized for her tardiness, and said that it was due to the treacherous conditions of the icy roads. Lyn then gave Shirley instructions on how to put on the outfit.

Shirley rushed to the back of the room to get dressed because we only had 30-minutes before show time began. When Shirley walked back to the front of the room, the room grew silent. It was an unbelievable fashion disaster.

Lyn was supposed to design a two-piece suit, with the jacket having a high stand-up collar. It was supposed to be the look that made a bold fashion statement, giving the appearance of an exaggerated turned up collar. Instead, it looked like an oversized alien's costume that stood four inches above her head, and little over a foot wide. The heaviness of the three-inch-thick cushioned collar drooped on a diagonal angle backward as Shirley tried to move around in it. When the collar fell backwards, the Velcro snaps that held the front of the jacket closed, immediately popped opened, completely exposing Shirley's bra and stomach. It was a complete disaster.

Shirley stood before us, as her eyes filled with tears.

Claudine composed herself, then said, "The show must go on. We are going to make this work the best way we can. That's why I told you to bring a back-up outfit, Shirley, but we can't worry about that now. We have fifteen minutes before show time. Now, it's all about your confidence. So, let's hurry up and finish, we have an audience of people out there anticipating this show. We have to give them our best. They've paid for a hair show, and were going to give them one to remember."

The first half of the show went off without a glitch. Three of my sisters were models and they represented me well. My sister, Vanessa was pregnant at the time and didn't feel well enough to participate. Gail was one of my models in the short-hair category. She worked the crowd over with her short and edgy haircut, along with her beauty and charm, as she walked the runway and had the audience in an uproar. Once Gail had gotten to the edge of the stage, she blew the audience a kiss. Then she turned and strutted her long legs, and perfectly wide hips back to the middle of the stage and finished out the routine with the rest of the short-hair models.

My sisters Juanita and Lakeisha modeled in the Caribbean scene together. Donnie McClurkin's *"I Got My Mind Made Up,"* played as they modeled. This category was right up Lakeisha's alley. She had very close Jamaican friends that she had convinced from the time she was in high school that she was half-Jamaican. She told them that she had a different father from the rest of us, and that he was Jamaican. Which was only part of the truth. She did have a different father from the four of us, but he was not Jamaican. He was an African-American man that she met for the first time when she was fourteen.

Juanita and Lakeisha added some extra Jamaican flare to the pre-choreographed routine, as they put extra movement in their hips. They showed the audience what true Caribbean dancing was all about.

Juanita threw her hands up in the air and began to hype the crowd as she strutted down the runway. As she turned to walk back to the middle of the stage, Lakeisha was approaching the runway to display my creative work. Both of them were so engrossed in the music that they high-fived each other as they exchanged positions on the stage. Although it was not a part of the rehearsed routine, it flowed as if they had practiced it for months. The audience cheered them on for their A-plus performance.

Clayton was the first on program, to perform during the intermission. I quickly ran and changed into my second outfit so I could be out there in time to see his performance. I just knew that all of the money that I'd invested in his music would finally pay off. His performance was the perfect opportunity for Clayton to develop a following, and all who heard him would inquire about purchasing his gospel CD. That would put the pressure on him to complete the CD faster.

I sat in the front row on the edge of my seat. Clayton gave the CD with his instrumentals on it to the sound technician, who'd started playing it before Clayton was ready to sing.

Clayton motioned for him to start the music over. I could see that Clayton's confidence was as low as the sound of the music on his soundtrack. He looked like a lost and scared puppy as he fought hard not to burst out crying in defeat in front of the audience.

My heart dropped as I watched the musical disaster unfold. The crowd paid him no attention and began to socialize, eat, and drink like he was invisible on the stage. That was the very reason Claudine wanted to hear his demo prior to the day of the show. All of the music was supposed to be brought to the sound technician to make sure that it was ready to be played on the sound system. Perhaps with Clayton only listening to his music through his headphones, he didn't realize just how low the sound was.

Clayton fumbled with the keyboard and you could tell he was struggling to hear the music. Both Claudine and I watched in shock. However, I didn't have time to wallow in disappointment and anger at my wasted effort to invest in Clayton's musical dream. Nor did I have time to try to encourage my very discouraged husband. The show had to carry on.

After Clayton's failed performance, I rushed back to our suite to touch-up my models' hair for the second half of the show. I quickly finished their hair, and as I was in the mirror fixing my own hair to model in the long and sleek hair category, Clayton walked into the room with an attitude.

"I'm leaving and going home. Are you coming?"

I looked at him like he was crazy. How selfish of him, that he would try to rain on my parade just because his performance went sour.

"No. I'm not. I'm sorry that your performance didn't turn out like you wanted, but I put a lot of hard work into this hair show, and I'm going to see it through to the end with or without you." I fought the urge to tell him it was his own fault for not letting us hear the music beforehand.

Clayton walked away with an attitude, but for once, I didn't care.

I walked out on stage and took my position with the rest of the models as we waited for Kirk Franklin's *"Brighter Day"* song to play. Once the music came on, all of the models high-stepped like stallions, using the same foot as we trotted to the beat of the rhythm. We did a routine, swinging our hair back and forth to mesmerize the crowd. It was my turn to high step it, all the way down the runway to show off my own work before the crowd. They went crazy over my whole ensemble. I stopped at the bottom of the stage, put my hands on my hips, and stepped each of my legs out to the side to the beat of the song to open up my stance. I did *the body check test*, as I shook my head from left to right to get the crowd's approval. I was on cloud nine as cheers reverberated throughout the room.

I turned and high-stepped back up to the middle of the

stage with the rest of the models. When we closed out the routine, we all took a bow as our long hair practically swept the floor.

When I stood up and looked out into the crowd, I spotted Clayton staring at me in anger. I was too excited with the success of the show, to be concerned with how unhappy he was.

When the show wrapped up, every stylist that participated took a bow. Since our salon was the hosting salon, we were the last to be introduced.

Backstage Claudine said, "Ruby, I want you to walk out there with me. I don't know what to do, I'm so nervous."

"No problem, you know that I have your back."

"Okay, I'm going to follow your lead."

Shirley was the first to walk out to represent our salon. She tried to walk out as cautiously as possible in an effort to balance the heavy and oversized collar. It worked very briefly, and then gravity took its course and pulled the heavy collar towards the ground. Shirley felt it falling and grabbed the front of the jacket, clutching it closed, just before the last couple of Velcro snaps popped open and exposed her in front of the crowd. She walked back to the middle of the stage holding the top of her jacket together, and waited for Claudine and me to take the runway. Claudine and I walked together, hand and hand, from the middle of the stage to the bottom of the runway and took our bow.

Claudine wore a beautiful emerald green gown. Her voluminous curly hair flowed perfectly, a little past her shoulders. There were two eras that stood before the audience in unity, hand-in-hand. We had managed to pull off a magnificent hair show, and the crowd showed their satisfaction with a standing ovation.

I should have been exhausted as I made my way home, but my adrenaline kept me wide awake.

"Mom, I missed you."

"I missed you, too, Son."

"You did a good job for the hair show."

"Thank you, Son. You are Mommy's biggest fan. Now let's hurry into the house so you can get ready to go to bed so you'll be well rested for school in the morning. That is, if it's not cancelled because of the weather."

I left all of my belongings in the car to quickly get out of the severely cold weather. "Come on, let's hurry inside."

"Okay, Mom."

I held his hand as we crossed the parking lot to go inside.

The weather had gotten worse and snow was pelting us. However, I knew the greater storm that I had to deal with was waiting on the other side of the door of our apartment, and I didn't know if I had the strength to weather it.

CHAPTER ELEVEN

"Come on, Ty. We have to get out of this weather and into shelter." I told my son as I began to shiver after hours of standing outside of the Chevron in the cold rain of Harvey.

"Yes, Mom. I know, but there is nowhere to go. All of the streets and freeways surrounding us are under water. We are basically trapped."

One of my son's close friends called him and was keeping him posted on what was on the local news. He told him that ninety percent of Dickinson was under water. We had just moved to Dickinson almost three months prior to Harvey.

"Son, the only place that we can go in to get out of this cold rain is-"

Before I could finish my sentence, my son interrupted me. "Oh no, Mom. We are not going in a funeral home to wait to be picked up."

"There are only two options. We could cross this street, and walk alive into the funeral home and wait inside, away from the elements of this nasty weather. Or, we could continue to wait outside and risk our lives by being totally exposed to the elements of this harsh and unpredictable weather, and then possibly be brought to the funeral home cold and stiff."

My son sighed. "All right, Mom, we'll go and wait in the funeral home, but we have to cross this street, which is now a river, and the current looks pretty strong. I'll lead the way. Hold on to the back of my jacket."

"Okay, but I need you to take the end of this sheet again, just in case I slip under."

My son looked at me and said, "Mom, you don't have to worry. You're not going to fall under, just don't let go of my jacket."

Holding a small plastic storage trunk with only a few of our belongings in it, along with the end of the fitted sheet that was tightly secured around my waist, my son slowly led the way into the water. I held on tightly to his jacket and followed his lead. It was so difficult to walk in the water because we had no clue of what was beneath our feet. We didn't know if we were stepping off of a curb, or whether the ground elevated or declined. Plus, the surrounding bayous had overflowed and snakes, alligators or other unknown creatures could've been lurking below the surface of the water.

I prayed as we walked through the water. *"Lord, have mercy on us. I could now see the frustration of the children of Israel. The Red Sea in front of them and Pharaoh's army closing in on them. Their options were few, if at all any. They had no choice but to go forward into the water. It's amazing that God would use the same man who was rescued from a wooden basket in the river as a baby, to bring others out of the water to safety. The same water that was supposed to drown him, he survived. His testimony of survival validated him enough to be able to bring others out of the water. He was not intimidated by it anymore. He had overcome it at an early age. The wood that formed a waterproof ark saved baby Moses' life. God chose to use the same substance to save other's lives as Moses held his wooden rod out against the water. It pushed the water back and made a barrier between the Israelites and the Red Sea. That same piece of wood in the shape of a T, came between the wrath of God and you and me. For we were all drowning profusely in the sea of our sins. Jesus stretched out his hands on that piece of wood called the cross and died, so that we could live. So Lord, I look for your deliverance as we cross this river that stands before us. Lord, please deliver us from this water!"*

I had to put on my big girl girdle, and suck it up until we made it to the other side of the street. The current pulled and tugged on my legs, as if we were in a tug of war match together. The more it pulled against me, the stronger I flexed my leg muscles to resist it, and planted my feet firmly on the ground beneath me.

The water was just about waist deep, as we reached the middle of the street. When we made it into the parking lot of the funeral home, the water was right at our knees. The closer we walked to the door of the building, the water had become more shallow. The funeral home was sitting on a hill, so even though the water covered the steps leading to the entrance of the building, it did not come inside.

I never thought I would be glad to be approaching a funeral home. There was an eerie feeling as we treaded through the water. It looked like a long funeral procession, as people lined up outside of the building underneath the canopy on both sides of the door. The funeral home was open and allowing people to go inside. My mind had begun to play tricks on me. It told me that being inside of a funeral home was a sign that we were not going to survive Harvey. I felt as if we were walking into our own doom, and that the funeral home would be our final destination.

I prayed within myself for our rescue to come quickly. The funeral home was a single-level building, so if it started to flood, none of us would have anywhere to escape. It would have become a massive grave site for all of us who were in there. The inside was filled to capacity with standing room only. Some families sat together in chairs, some cuddled on the floor, holding their little ones close while trying to keep them calm. If seemed as if the entire city of Dickinson was dropped off at the funeral home and was waiting to be brought to shelter. There were elderly people who were exhausted. They mustered up what little strength left within them to hold their feeble bodies upon the chairs they were in. People who had health challenges were dragging oxygen tanks along with them just hoping they'd soon be brought to shelter. Not to forget the different breeds of furry four legged pets, both dogs and cats, that crowded in with their owners and the rest of us. We all were exhausted from waiting.

Full-size pickup trucks, with gigantic wheels, started moving people out of the funeral home and into various shelters. However, people were continuously being rescued out of their flooded homes and dropped off at the funeral home. No sooner than they moved people out to be brought into shelter, the faster they dropped more people off who were rescued from their flooded homes. And so, the funeral home stayed full to capacity. Naturally, they were taking the sick, elderly, and children first with one parent to accompany them, so I had no idea how long it would be before my son and I got a chance to be brought to shelter.

Night was beginning to fall, and I didn't want it to catch us at the funeral home. We walked outside to see if we could squeeze into one of the trucks that was transporting people to the shelter at a middle school in League City, but there was no room.

I was desperate to get out of the funeral home, especially before nightfall. If water had come into the funeral home while we slept, there would have been nowhere for us to escape. The funeral home would have become an instant one-story pool of death.

I had to think quickly.

"Son, the next truck that has room available for us, we are getting in it no matter what direction it is going," I said. As we waited outside, a red full-size pickup truck, with monster wheels stopped in front of the building.

"Does anyone need to go to Texas City?" the driver yelled. No one was jumping at his offer.

"Come on, Ty. Let's get on this truck, before nightfall," I said.

"Mom, are you sure? Do you know anybody who lives in Texas City? We won't be out of the clear if we go there," he replied.

Texas City, was going farther towards Galveston Island. For the evacuees who waited at the funeral home, it was going in the opposite direction that we all wanted to go in. We were trying to go farther inland to get far away from the water. Although, we didn't know at the time that the places that normally would have received the most flooding like Galveston Island, received little to no flooding.

One news reporter said, "It's as if Harvey has played a game of hopscotch all over the city of Houston." We all were unsure of what area he would land on. Harvey was a beast that we had never seen before as he took a long and grueling tour of our city. Just when we thought Harvey was leaving, he doubled back to visit some of the scenery that he had missed, as he moved at the speed of two-miles-per-hour.

I looked into my son's eyes and said, "Look, we have no other choice. Just trust me, we will be okay. God is going to take care of us."

The people in the truck called out one last time. "Hey, is there anyone who is going to Texas City? We have room."

"Yes. We are!" I yelled.

We climbed on the back of the truck with a few male strangers. I was thankful that my son left the comfort of his dorm room to wait the storm out with me. I didn't know what could have possibly become of me, especially after jumping into the back of a stranger's pick-up truck, if he was not there.

We held each other's hand tightly as the truck pulled off. The farther we pulled away from the funeral home, the deeper the truck submerge into the murky water, even leveling out and floating at one point as if it had turned into a motor boat. None of the truck's wheels could visibly be seen as the water came midways up the truck. I prayed hard, hoping that the current of the water didn't flip the truck over.

There weren't any visible streets in sight, everything looked like one gigantic river. Street signs stood only two-feet high, as they peeked their necks out of the murky water. My heart started to sink as the sun set, and the uncertainty of where we were going began to give me anxiety.

The truck continued to plow through the murky water

until it emerged onto dry ground then slowed to a stop.

"What's going on?" I called out as the driver got out, walked around and pulled down the latch of the truck.

"This is the farthest that I can take you," he said, then pointed to a blue truck that was parked ahead of us. "The blue truck is going to take you to an overnight shelter in Texas City. The community has formed their own transportation system to bring people to shelter."

I was a little hesitant and reluctant to be transported into another truck, but we had no other choice. We were at the mercy of strangers and had to trust that they were going to do the right thing. I jumped down off of the truck first and my son followed me. We walked down the road to board the blue truck that waited for us. Once we had gotten in, there was a family that had two teenage sons, that gave up their seats in the rear of the truck so that my son and I wouldn't have to ride in the bed of the truck. The father drove, while the mother sat in the passenger seat.

"Y'all want some chips and water?" she asked.

We gladly accepted as the truck submerged into the murky water, and we sailed off with very little daylight left, in pursuit of shelter. This wasn't the first time that I traveled at night in a truck in pursuit of shelter.

The U-Haul was filled with just about everything we owned, with the exception of a few of my son's and my belongings, and Clayton's car attached to the back of it. We headed down I-95 with very little daylight left in pursuit of shelter. It was February of 2005. Clayton had decided to move down to Houston first to seek employment. I funded the entire relocation trip, and helped drive Clayton to Houston, with the assistance of his cousin.

My son stayed back at home with my mother and sisters for a week until we got Clayton moved and settled in Houston. I caught a flight back to Massachusetts and we remained there until my son finished out the school year. My son and I joined him in late June of that year.

Clayton said that Springfield was the cause of our marriage troubles, because of all the bad memories of his past that caused him to be so unhappy. My past hadn't been a bed of roses either, but I learned to find joy in the fact that my family had overcome what appeared to be the darkest hours of our lives by God's grace. Therefore, I decided to choose joy and victory, over sadness and defeat. I only hoped that Clayton would one day look at life from that perspective.

The move to Houston came as a surprise. Clayton simply woke up one morning and said that God was telling him to move our family to Houston. I was skeptical about relocating because Clayton still wasn't paying bills, except the for car insurance and the phone bill when he felt like it. I had a steady clientele at the shop and if I moved away to Houston, I would have to start my eight-year clientele all over. It would be challenging to build a clientele in Houston without knowing a soul there. I had a whole lot to lose by moving to Houston. Plus, I had a son to think about, and I knew that making money behind the styling chair was how I provided and took care of him.

Clayton had already proven that he was incapable of stepping up as the head of the household. So, I told Clayton that I wasn't going at first, and he would have to go by himself. However, I decided to go on a twenty-one-day consecration to seek God for direction—if I should go or stay. I didn't eat any food, or drink any water until seven in the evening.

After twenty-one days of fasting and crying out to God, I received my answer from Him. I was supposed to relocate with my husband. God let me know that I would go through more hard and tough times, but He would be with me, and bring me from the wilderness to the promised land.

I told Clayton the news and he was overjoyed. "Honey, our marriage is going to flourish and be like it's brand new."

The problem that I had believing Clayton's words, was that our marriage was literally brand new. We had been married less than two years and I didn't think that a change in scenery could magically make it any better. The problems in our marriage ran deep within Clayton, and until he tried to change himself from the inside out, any exterior solution of happiness would only last momentarily. Clayton's solution was to run from everything he did not like, or if things did not particularly go his way.

Right before the move, Clayton told me that the Lord was calling him to preach the gospel. I was elated to hear the news because I knew that sermons always minister to the one delivering it first. I quickly ran to the Christian bookstore and bought Clayton his first study bible. He asked me to purchase a black clergy shirt, the one with the white collar. He wanted the appearance of an authentic minister. Clayton didn't realize that a clergy shirt wasn't going to make him act right or even preach right for that matter. Clayton lacked the heart to treat people how he wanted to be treated, in addition to the discipline to "study to show himself approved unto God."

So it was no surprise when his first sermon was a big flop.

No one could make heads or tails out of it. I wanted to go underneath the church pew out of embarrassment. I didn't expect his first sermon to be perfect, but I expected him at least to put forth an effort into studying. I wanted his sermon to make sense. But the study bible had sat on the shelf of our closet while collecting dust until a day or two before he had to deliver the Word. Shortly after Clayton gave his first sermon at his parents' church, he told me that we were leaving there and moving to his brother's church, which was more modernized. I wasn't particularly in favor of leaving his parents church but, as the submissive wife that I was, I had to follow my husband.

Clayton's brother was a bishop, and a dynamic and gifted preacher of his congregation. When he brought the word, everyone was always engaged and on the edge of their seats, eager to hear more. He'd often brought the crowds to their feet, with the energetic and expository way that he brought the Word to life. He had everything that it took to be a great leader. I was hopeful that what Clayton's brother had, would somehow rub off on him.

I guess Clayton wanted to broaden his horizons and preach, since his musical endeavors weren't exactly taking off as he thought they should have. Especially after his failed performance at the hair show. Clayton's brother wanted to take him under his wing to mentor and groom him to be a minister. However, Clayton had a hard time taking directions from anyone, especially if he wasn't in charge.

Once, Clayton got up and stormed out of the church while his brother was in the middle of teaching bible study, because he didn't agree with what was being said. I was afraid that Clayton was about to make the decision to leave his brother's church. I had quickly fell in love with his theologically enriched teachings, and began to grow so much in my walk with Christ. I learned to take God outside of the perimeter walls of the denominational beliefs, that were so deeply integrated into my thought patterns. For example, I wore pants for the first time since my conversion to Christ, as I learned that wearing them weren't going to send me to hell. I also began to wear make-up to enhance the beauty that God had already given me. It was if I had been reborn again. For the first time in a long time, I felt like I was coming into my own self-awareness, and could be the true authentic me. I was so relieved when Clayton decided not to leave his brother's church. Clayton had received his license to be a minister just before he moved to Houston.

I continued to go to church while I waited for my son to finish school. Clayton's brother told me that he wanted me to bring the Word on the Sunday before I moved to Houston. The message was entitled "I'm Coming Out of the Fire." It was ironic that as I delivered that particular message, there was a firehouse parade in the area, and a procession of fire trucks sounded their sirens non-stop. However, I was determined to keep on going through the distractions of the loud sirens.

To my surprise, Clayton's brother licensed and ordained me that Sunday, immediately after I concluded the message. I wondered if the fire trucks sounding off their sirens was symbolic of God rescuing me out of the fiery troubles that I faced in my marriage? *Perhaps being away from Clayton for a few months would have given him enough time to miss and appreciate me,* I thought.

I soon learned that wasn't the case. I was about to enter into the fiery furnace of my life. Not even all the fire trucks that sounded their sirens the day I delivered my last message at Clayton's brother's church, would be able to put out the ferocious flames.

I said my final farewells and goodbyes to all of my family and friends, and filled my car up to capacity with me and my son's belongings, since I was paying for my car to be shipped to Houston. Clayton's father brought us to the airport on June 27, 2005. We'd decided to take Clayton's sixteen-year-old nephew, Michael along with us to give him a fresh start. He was a good kid overall, but had started hanging out with the wrong crowd and began to get into some trouble. We wanted to take the burden off of Clayton's parents so that they wouldn't have to exert their energy to try to get his life back on track.

As the plane began to take off down the runway, my son closed his eyes and grabbed my hand and squeezed it, as he didn't like the feeling of taking off and landing. I whispered in his ear, "It's going to be all right. Soon it will be smooth sailing and we'll be gliding far above the clouds."

CHAPTER TWELVE

    The eagle is a symbol of strength, by its capability to soar far above the storm. The eagle uses the wind beating against its wings as momentum to catapult him far into the atmosphere, giving it the ability to soar on top of the wind. There are storms in life that will beat so violently against you, until they knock out what little bit of wind you thought you had left within. So then, how was I expected to soar far above the storms that came violently against me? I was depleted of the wind that comes from within, to give me momentum and strength to rise above the storm.

    As blackness filled the night's air, and the rain continued to fall heavily all over Houston, I found myself wishing that my son and I had wings of eagles to carry us far above the storm of Harvey.

    We sailed down the street in the blue pick-up truck, trying to make it to the shelter in Texas City. As the driver continued to reroute in order to maneuver around the high flood waters that we encountered, I wasn't sure if we were going to make it to see another day. However, the driver was determined and we finally arrived safe and sound.

My son and I thanked the driver, and his family. There was a cop who stood in front of the shelter, as we approached the it.

"This is not an overnight shelter. I am asking everyone to leave now," He said.

"What do you mean this is not an overnight shelter?" I asked. "Why are people getting instructions to bring us here?"

"Look, I know that you're frustrated," the officer said. "But we don't have the set-up for this to be an overnight shelter. We don't have the capacity to fit people in here properly, nor the equipment such as beds."

"Look, I just want us to get out of the cold rain. It's dark and we don't have anywhere to go. What about that middle school right over there? Why can't you open it up to get all of these people in out of the rain?"

"I'm sorry, but we just don't have the funds to open up the middle school."

A feeling of hopelessness consumed me. "Then I don't know what we are going to do," I said, my voice quivered.

Just then, a man approached us. "There is an overnight shelter set up at Abundant Life Christian Center in Texas City. I could bring the both of you over there."

We were at the point of desperation, so we quickly took him up on his offer and climbed into his truck. Just then, my cell phone rang. It was one of my friends who was concerned about us because the news had revealed just how bad the flooding was in Dickinson. I told her what was going on, and she asked me did I know anyone who lived in the Texas City area, that I could call to stay over their house for a few days. I thought of two of my clients/friends who lived in the area. The first person I called had no flooding inside of her home, but the neighborhood she lived in was surrounded by water, so that no one could get in or no one could leave out. I called the other friend and found out that her area wasn't flooded.

I asked the driver if he could bring us to the dog track, which was right down the street from Theresa's house, and she would meet us there.

I was relieved to see a familiar face. It gave me joy as if I had hit the lottery. I thanked her over and over as I shivered in the front seat of her car.

"Girl, you don't have to keep on thanking me. I know that you would have done the same for me and my son. We are all in this together," she said.

When we made it into her house, my son and I embraced, grateful that we survived Hurricane Harvey, even though the storm wasn't quite over.

My friend Theresa, allowed us to wash our clothing that was soiled from being out in the contaminated floodwater. My son got into the shower to change out of his wet clothing first. I hesitated momentarily to get into the shower. The thought of more water falling on me had sent a flutter of anxiety through me. However, I soon dismissed that temporary fear, and forced myself into the shower to wash away the awful residue of the storm, and to cleanse my mind and body from the stress of it all. As I showered, I cried and thanked God for bringing us to safety.

After I showered and got dressed, I went into the living room to watch the news. I was finally able to see just how widespread the storm really was, and the magnitude of it was jaw-dropping. I learned that people all throughout Houston had gone through similar situations as my son and me, and for some far worse. My heart broke as I learned of the lives that were lost during the storm. Those who lost their lives, while fighting to save their own lives, and the lives of others, died fighting to survive. I viewed them as warriors and heroes.

As we continued to watch the news, we sat there in awe, humbled and grateful at the same time that we made it out with our lives. We were not fully aware of all that we lost at our flooded home, nor did it seem to matter at that moment, for we had one another.

On the other hand, it just always seemed like I was constantly facing an upward battle in my life, no matter how hopeful I was to see better days ahead of me. I seemed to always get set back.

CHAPTER THIRTEEN

I was hopeful that my absence from Clayton would've made his heart grow fonder toward me, and that our dysfunctional marriage would miraculously become functional, for the betterment of our family.

Clayton had greeted me at the airport like he was excited to see me. I was overly excited to see him, too. It had been a little over four months since the last time I saw him. I earnestly desired to reunite with Clayton in every sense of the way. It had been such a long time since my husband made love to me. I just didn't know what I could do to make him desire me. I thought for sure that before I left to go back home after helping him relocate to Houston that February, he would have made passionate love to me, to give me something to think about while we were apart. It simply did not happen. I guess because the time frame didn't fit into Clayton's annual love making schedule.

When Clayton could no longer convince me that God was causing him not to desire me because of our disobedience in not doing ministry adequately, he blamed it on the city that we grew up in. Clayton believed that people in our hometown were working witchcraft on him, that caused him to be impotent in order to destroy our marriage. He was so convinced that when he left Springfield, it lifted the curse off of him. He often told me when we talked over the phone before I joined him in Houston, he was going to "tear me up" after I arrived, and make love to me constantly. Well, the time had come to see if our marriage would make an about face forward into love and happiness.

We all squeezed into Clayton's car from the airport like we were sardines, after we crammed our luggage into his car and headed down the I-45 South Gulf Freeway, in pursuit of our new life in Houston. My son and Clayton's nephew excitingly pointed out all of the new and unfamiliar restaurants that we passed. Clayton chimed in on all of the wonderful restaurants that he wanted to take us to. There was such a newness in the atmosphere that initiated a new beginning for us all, and we were all optimistic of what the future held for us.

As Clayton exited the freeway into the Clear Lake area, we were on the home stretch to get to our apartment. We were just in awe of the beautiful palm trees that were planted on an island of landscaping, right in the middle of Bay Area Blvd. that added a vacation like feel to the place. I had planned on taking two months off before I started working again. I had worked vigorously to try to make all of the money that I possibly could before I left Springfield. However, I had set myself up for failure, since I was responsible for paying the rent in Springfield, as well as in Houston. Clayton had found a job working at Foley's, in the women's shoe department. He said that he just wasn't making enough money there to pay the bills. That's why I had to take on the financial responsibility of the apartment in Houston, too.

It wasn't until two months before I moved to Houston, that I got some financial relief. Clayton's parents allowed my son and me to stay with them free of charge. I wasn't sure how we were going to survive financially while I built my clientele in Houston. However, I was a woman of faith, and believed that the Lord would provide for us somehow.

We pulled up to our apartment and unloaded our suitcases and dragged them up a flight of stairs and into our second floor apartment. My son looked around in excitement, and immediately identified his bedroom, by his bed and belongings. He rushed into the bedroom and plopped onto his bed to reacquaint himself with it. His arms and hands moved up and down the comforter like he was in the snow, making a snow angel. His hands and fingertips caressed every fiber of the fabric underneath them.

"Hey, I want to take Michael to see some of the beautiful attractions of Houston. Let's go to Kemah Boardwalk. What do you say, Ruby? You all want to go?"

"Yes!" the kids exclaimed. But I had reservations about the money that would be spent for all four of us to be entertained at the Kemah Boardwalk. Clayton did not realize how financially draining the move really was because I footed the cost of everything. He was totally oblivious to the sacrifice that I made to make his vision of relocating, a reality. However, I agreed, and we all had a blast and enjoyed all that Kemah had to offer. We finished the night with dinner at one of the exquisite restaurants on the waterfront.

We made our way back to the apartment for the night, and the boys showered, then went to bed. I was exhausted and took a nice long shower as well. I adorned my body with enticing body lotion, and the scent of seductive and sweet smelling perfume—the same bedtime regiment I used to try to pique my husband's interest. I wanted to be irresistible to Clayton. I wanted him to have me like the dinner that he had just eaten at Landry's Seafood House. Although it was an extremely long day, I was never too exhausted to give myself to my husband.

    I couldn't imagine that Clayton would reject me that day, because he had time to actually miss me. He was already under the covers fast asleep with the a/c unit on Artic blast, so I decided to bring the heat. There was no need for me to put a piece of clothing on my body. Only the warm feel of my soft and silky caramel skin to wrap around his, would be suitable for this type of family reunion.

    I slowly climbed into the bed, totally unbothered by the frigid air that blew out from the vents, and crawled underneath the covers. I pushed my body up against his and threw my leg over him, and massaged his lower extremities with my thigh, as I caressed his chest. I then mounted Clayton and kissed his lips as he laid there in a comatose state until he couldn't take it anymore, and slid me off to the side of him. He turned on his side with his back facing me, curled up in a fetal position with his hands tucked between his legs and said, "I'm tired. It's been a long day, and you should be tired, too."

    I wanted to scream! I was beyond fed up, hurt, and disappointed by Clayton's constant rejection of me—I was pissed off. I had to quickly get out of the bed, and put on some clothing to go into the living room to pray and cool down, as my emotions had gotten the best of me. I cried in silence, while on my knees so that I did not wake up my son and nephew.

"*Here I am Lord, once again, crying out to You about the same issue,*" I prayed. "*I don't know what else to do. I thought that You were going to make it better between us. Lord, please change my husband's heart toward me so that he can love me. Please give him the desire to want to be with me. Lord, since you have not removed this thorn from me, this issue of no intimacy in my marriage, please grant me the grace to bear it. I look to you, God for strength, for you are the author and the finisher of my faith.*"

I headed back to the room, climbed back into bed, and curled up on my side in a fetal position, softly rocking myself to sleep as the tears saturated my pillow.

A month had gone by since we reunited with Clayton in Houston, and his attitude toward me seemed to have gotten worse. Clayton wanted me to buy him a piece of musical equipment that served as a home music studio. It was expensive, and I didn't have enough money to cover the entire cost of it. I had started working in a salon that Clayton had found for me before I left to join him in Houston, that was right down the street from our apartment. He wanted to make sure that I had a place to work so that I could quickly build up my clientele. I had hoped to take some time off, but Clayton quickly complained about how hard it was on him to pay rent the first month after I got there. So, I immediately went back to work two weeks after I arrived in Houston.

Clayton didn't understand that it was going to take some time to build my clientele. In addition to helping Clayton with July's rent, I was using the little bit of money that I saved to buy groceries along with the miscellaneous things that we all needed at the house. When I told Clayton that I didn't have the money to cover the entirety of the equipment, it didn't sit well with him.

"You stayed in my mother's house rent free and you have the nerve not to bring enough money down here. You were supposed to be putting away all of the money, so that you can come down here and contribute to the bills," he snapped.

I could not believe my ears. Had Clayton *really* forgotten, that I was the main contributor to paying all of the bills in our dysfunctional and loveless marriage up until I relocated? I did not know how much money he expected me to have, after I carried the load of everything because he was incapable of doing it.

"I did the best that I could to save money, but it was not easy with the responsibility of paying the rent for two apartments," I cried.

"I don't want to hear that," he said. "You knew what we were going to be up against moving here, with you having to build your clientele. You should have prepared better for it," he barked.

"Clayton, I don't believe you," I said. "I am doing, and have done, the best that I possibly can, and you're being unreasonable. I went back to work after two weeks of being here, after almost working myself into the ground before I left, to make things work. I am exhausted and was supposed to take the rest of the summer off until the boys started school, but I'm doing everything in my power to make this move work for our family."

"Well, you're not doing enough. So, you're just going to sit on your butt and watch the bottom fall out of everything, and let it crumble to pieces. I can't swing all of this by myself. I need this piece of musical equipment so that I can make some extra money producing beats for people. One of us has to make some money around here!"

I was beyond hurt by the words that came out of Clayton's mouth, and his selfishness that had blinded him to all of the sacrifices that I made for him.

"I am not just sitting on my butt," I said. "I go to work every day, trying to build a clientele, but it takes time. No one knows me out here, that's why I've made business cards and fliers to pass out to people. I have gotten put out of the mall for soliciting while trying to pass them out, so that people can know where I work and what I specialize in. Although, people are not going to just sit in a stranger's chair based off of a flier or business card alone. It's going to take me actually doing people's hair, so that they can spread the word about me. That's why it is vital for me to be in the salon every day just in case a walk-in comes through. I don't know what else you expect me to do. I have filled out applications at Walmart, McDonalds, and Target, to try to work part-time while building my clientele, but none of those places have called me back."

Clayton looked at me as if everything I said to him went over his head. "Do you have any money left? I really need this piece of equipment."

"I only have six-hundred-dollars left to my name. I could only contribute four hundred of that, because I need to spend the rest on groceries."

"I'll take that, and figure the rest out."

I begrudgingly gave the four hundred dollars to Clayton, not knowing when I would earn it back at the salon. I just wanted the argument to end.

Just then, there was a knock on our bedroom door, it was

Clayton's nephew.

"Hey Uncle Clayton, I have some money that I saved that could cover the cost of your musical equipment."

Michael had overheard us arguing and wanted to help bring some peace into the 800 square ft. apartment.

"No, Michael, that's your money. You shouldn't have to spend it on me." Clayton looked at me with disgust as he continued. "We should have had enough money coming down here. That's why your Aunt Ruby was staying at my mother's house rent free."

"Uncle Clayton, it's all right, you can take the money. I don't mind helping. How much do you need?"

"Well, Ruby has four hundred of it, and I have two hundred. All I need is six hundred dollars."

"Okay, I have it."

Clayton's parents sent Michael with some money so that he could take care of himself and not be a financial burden on us.

"Thank you so much, Michael. I really feel bad taking this money from you. You are my nephew, and I didn't bring you down here for this. I'm supposed to be helping you get your life back on track, not you helping me."

"Uncle Clayton, you know we go way back. You were there for me when I was little. We are family, and that's what family is for, to lean on each other in times of need."

Clayton smiled with pride. "Get dressed, nephew. I want you to come with me to get the equipment. It's very nice. I'm going to teach you how to make beats on it."

Michael raced into his room to get ready and my son grabbed his shoes to go with them.

"I want to go, too."

"Me and Michael are taking care of business, we'll be right back," Clayton said.

My son pouted in disappointment. So, I decided to take him to the park after they left. As he played at the jungle gym, I sat on the park bench deep in thought. Clayton did not thank me once, for contributing the last bit of my hard earned money to help him purchase his musical equipment. And the nerve of him to have excluded my son from going with them. Tyquon viewed Clayton as a father figure, especially since he left his biological father in Massachusetts. Tyquon's father didn't try to make an effort to maintain a relationship with his son once we moved to Houston.

It didn't take long before my son was drenched in sweat, and exhausted from playing in the extreme heat of the Texas sun. I handed him an ice cold bottle of water and wiped his face with a towel. I felt horrible that I could not give him any other relief from the heat. My a/c in my car didn't work and I didn't have the money to get it repaired. I should have invested the four hundred dollars in fixing my a/c unit, instead of giving it to Clayton. It's sad to say, I had rather dealt with the heat than to deal with the flames of Clayton's nasty attitude.

By the time we got to the grocery store, our clothing was glued to us with sweat. Clayton was totally unbothered when he saw his family dragging into the house from the sweat box of my car, almost on the verge of having a heat stroke.

My son and I rushed into Food Town, a discounted grocery store, to get some relief from the heat. I stocked up on meat and bought Zip-lock freezer bags, so that I could repackage the meat for our family of four, to be ready to pull it from the freezer as needed. I bought plenty of rice and beans to stretch our meals. I could no longer afford to buy fresh fruits and vegetables, with the exception of onions and bell peppers to help season the food.

I put all that I needed in the carriage to make my son's favorite meal of spaghetti and meatballs, and refused to cut corners on the way he liked it. He had to adjust to so many changes with our move to Houston, and I did not want to change the way he knew and loved my spaghetti.

We left the grocery store and headed home so that I could prepare the dinner for my family. As I drove home, I realized that things had gotten beyond real, as the reality of spending the last of the money I had saved on groceries for my household set in. From that point forward, until I started seeing the financial increase from my clientele building up, we could no longer afford the luxury of dining out. I was on a tight budget, or rather, a faith-filled budget—not knowing how I would take care of my family, but believing that the Lord would make a way for us, somehow. I trusted Him to sustain us in the place He sent us to.

My son and I made a few trips from the car, and up the long flight of stairs to carry all of the groceries in. Sweat poured off of us as we tried hard to catch our breath from exerting ourselves in the heat. I went into the restroom to wash the sweat off of my face and to clean my hands to prepare the dinner.

"Ty, hurry up and wash your face and hands, so you can help me with the dinner," I called out to him.

"Okay, Mom. I'm coming."

When I began to cut up the bell peppers, garlic, and onions, the tears began to flow from my eyes. My heart ached from the reality that my loveless marriage was not getting any better. A change of scenery had not changed a thing. I had given Clayton my all, including the very last of my money, and he didn't show any signs of affection toward me. I was twenty-six-years-old, and far from the people who I knew genuinely loved my son and me, and had our best interest at heart.

My son walked into the kitchen with the palms of his hands turned up and said, "See, Mom. They're clean. What do you want me to do next?"

When I turned to him, he saw the tears falling.

"Mom, are you crying? Why are you crying?"

I sniffed. "I'm cutting up this onion and it has my eyes watering. Now move back before your eyes start watering, too."

I gathered myself together so I could finish cooking. I turned the burner up until the oil in the skillet bubbled up and made a sizzling sound like a large audience quickly clapping their hands for an encore. The more I fed the oil the onions, garlic and bell peppers, the louder it sizzled.

"Here you go, Son. Help me mix the seasoning into the hamburger. You have to squish it up really good, as I'm sprinkling it on the meat." Tyquon became tickled by the way the hamburger felt as it oozed through his fingers. He massaged and squeezed it as if it were play dough.

"That's good enough, Son. Now help me put it into the skillet to cook it," I said.

Clayton and Michael returned shortly after we finished with the dinner.

"Man, Aunt Ruby, it smells good in here. I am so hungry," Michael exclaimed as he inhaled the aroma from the food.

"I helped my mom cook everything. The spaghetti, the vegetables, and even the Italian bread that's still in the oven cooking," Tyquon said.

"I sure can't wait to test your cooking skills out, Tyquon," Michael replied.

Clayton didn't say a word as he opened up his equipment with a stale look on his face. I tried to break the silence with cordial conversation.

"Hey, Honey, is that the one that you anticipated getting?"

"Yes. This one will get the job done right now. But I'm going back when I have the money to purchase the other equipment I need."

"Well, I hope you're happy with *this* one right now," I said. "Your plate is on the table, and I don't want your food to get cold."

"Okay. I'll get it in a minute."

Clayton kept an attitude with me, throughout dinner and later, as we headed to bed. Clayton was on his side with his back to me. I eased into the bed and knew better than to lay a hand on him. So I silently laid there and cried myself to sleep, hoping that the morning would bring a brighter day.

CHAPTER FOURTEEN

I was awakened by the rays of the bright and beautiful sunlight that pierced through the blinds, and the conversations of the birds communicating their plans for the day as they chirped. Although it felt as though I had closed my eyes only moments ago, somehow I felt refreshed from the inspiration and hope of the sunlight that a brand new day brought.

I got up to pack Clayton's lunch from the previous night's dinner. Then I took the boys to get registered for school, as school was scheduled to start in two weeks. Tyquon was entering his third year of elementary school, while Michael was going into his junior year of high school.

Michael and Tyquon anticipated the start of school so they could make new friends in the new city they were in. I too, was anticipating the start of school, as I struggled to find things to keep the boys entertained. Not to mention, it was a struggle to keep both of them fed, three meals a day with little to no money.

With what little money I made at the salon while I was in the process of building my clientele, I tried to keep food in the refrigerator. Even still, things were extremely tight at the time. I looked through all of my old purses, coats and jackets that I wore in Massachusetts to try to find some loose dollars or change to purchase groceries for my family. After those were completely depleted of funds, in my desperation, I scrounged around for the forgotten about coins in the change pockets and underneath the seats of my car. To say the least, I was relieved when school started, so that my son and nephew could eat breakfast and lunch at school. I only had to worry about providing dinner for them after school was in session.

After I registered the boys for school, they spent the remainder of the day exerting their energy playing basketball. It was time to return home so they could eat dinner and go to sleep. I wanted them on a regular sleeping schedule two weeks prior to them starting school. They had to readjust to going to sleep at a decent time. I thought that a decent bedtime for Michael would be 10:30pm at the latest, since he had to be to school at 7:20am. Tyquon's bedtime was set for 8:30pm, or no later than 9:00pm.

We had eaten dinner, then watched what one of the three local television channels had to offer us since we could not afford cable. Shortly after, the time had come for my son to make his scheduled bedtime.

Clayton walked through the door without speaking to Michael and me. Although we spoke to him, he ignored us and quickly glanced at us before he stormed off into the bathroom and slammed the door shut in anger. I went to the door of the bathroom and spoke to Clayton door, "Hey, Honey, are you all right? Did something happen at work?"

He didn't answer me so I assumed that he must have had

a horrible day at work, so I thought to give him time to unwind and cool off. I went back into the living room and continued to watch television as I waited for him to come out of the bathroom. A few minutes later, he charged out of the bathroom and into the living room where Michael and I sat watching television.

"I just want y'all to know that I am not stupid," he snapped. "Y'all think you're pulling the wool over my eyes. I am not a fool!" he roared.

"Clayton, what's wrong with you? What are you talking about," I asked?

Clayton continued to gurgle up nonsense. "I have the spirit of discernment and I know that something is not right when I walked into this place tonight."

I became agitated with what Clayton tried to insinuate. "You need to stop talking in riddles and say plainly what you want to say, so there is no misunderstanding of what you *think* that you've discerned upon walking in here tonight."

Clayton said, "I can't believe that my nephew would betray me and be intimate with you, my wife!"

"What?" Michael exclaimed. He ended up storming out of the apartment, with tears in his eyes in total disbelief. Michael had the utmost love and respect for his uncle, and trusted him with his very life. I had gotten accustomed to the way Clayton treated me, but for him to drag Michael into his madness, had me beyond livid.

"No, you didn't go there! I treat this child as if he were my own flesh and blood, placing no difference between him and my own son. How dare you accuse me of sleeping with a sixteen-year-old boy! Just because you're not touching me doesn't mean that I would prey on a child. If I wanted to be trifling and cheat, I would have no problem walking outside and getting a full-grown man to fulfill my sexual needs and desires. Don't think for one moment just because you don't want me in that way, that I would have a problem getting a full-grown adult man, if that's what I wanted to do. I tell men on a daily basis that I am married when they approach me, so don't get it twisted, Clayton. You better be grateful that I'm really saved, and that I'm faithful to God first, even before being faithful to your loveless, mean, and coldhearted behind. That's what keeps me grounded and sane in this craziness of a marriage that I'm in with you." I took a deep breath to calm down.

"Now look what you have done! It's late and dark and you have this boy out wandering the streets because you have broken his heart."

"Whatever. I know that I'm right!"

I ignored his crazy accusation momentarily, to go outside to look for Michael. I walked across the street to the park to see if he was there, but he wasn't. By the time I walked back to the apartments I saw Michael sitting on the bottom of the stairs, his eyes red from crying. I sat on the stairs beside him.

"Michael, I am so sorry that your uncle accused you of such an unmentionable deed with me. I am really embarrassed and hurt for him. I know how much it hurts you because you love and look up to him as a role model."

More tears began to run down Michael's face and he quickly wiped them away in anger. "I lost all respect for my uncle tonight. He'd better stay far away from me, if he knows what's best for him. I'm not a little kid anymore and I'm not going to sit back and let him disrespect me. He wants to talk to me like a man from the streets, so I could give it to him like a man from the streets."

I quickly interjected, "Michael, he is still your uncle, and I'm not going to allow that to happen."

"No! I'm not going to allow anyone to disrespect me, blood or no blood, uncle or not. He doesn't appreciate anything you do, Aunt Ruby. You've spent the very last of your money to help him get that home music studio, and the whole time while we were out getting it, he was talking bad about you not coming down here with enough money. You try to do everything to make us all happy and he doesn't appreciate it. I feel so bad for you, he's always fussing and complaining about everything you do."

I patted his arm. "Don't worry about me, Michael. God has built me strong to take it. That's why you hear me praying all of the time because I believe that God will change your uncle to become more of a loving person. You have to forgive him, and pray for him, too."

Michael shook his head. "Aunt Ruby, I will never disrespect you, but my uncle better stay as far away from me as possible, or else."

"I understand that you are upset right now, and you have every right to be. Please just come inside and try to lay down and go to sleep. And perhaps some of your anger will subside. I know that after I've had a hard night, I pray myself to sleep, and when I wake up in the morning I feel a little better."

"All right Aunt Ruby, I just need five more minutes by myself out here, before I go back inside," he replied.

"All right, only five more minutes. We are in a new city, and I don't want anything bad to happen to you out here."

I went back inside and into our bedroom. I had put on a

good face for Michael, but I was livid. Just when I thought that Clayton could go no lower, he never ceased to amaze me. Clayton let his own insecurities and paranoia over the fact that he was not sleeping with me, lead him to accuse his nephew of something so egregious.

I closed my eyes in anger and bitterness that night. My heart also bled for Michael, because I knew how much his uncle's false accusations tore him up inside.

Things weren't quite the same between Michael and Clayton, for the remainder of the time he stayed with us in Houston. Michael had lost all hope of turning his life around after that encounter with his uncle.

When school began, he immediately started skipping classes, even though Clayton or I would drop him off every morning. It wasn't long before we began to get a couple of high fines from the truancy officers at Michael's school. Clayton and his parents decided that it was time for Michael to move back home with them, as we couldn't afford to pay the fines. Clayton never could see the negative impact that his emotional issues had on the people around him. He was constantly insulting and hurting those closest to him, and then would play the victim role. I was constantly warring and praying in the spirit for Clayton to become the man that God wanted him to be, so in turn, he could become the husband that I envisioned him to be. But my prayers seemed to have brought on more hurt and grief, along with long sleepless and loveless nights. I continued to wonder how long I was to endure the pain.

CHAPTER FIFTEEN

I wondered how long it would be before I could go back home to make an assessment of the damage that the storm, Hurricane Harvey caused? As hospitable and accommodating as my friend was in opening up her home to us during the storm, I was ready to go home to face the devastation in order to begin the rebuilding process. My friend, Theresa, drove me to Walmart early that Wednesday morning. That was the day the stores had just reopened after the storm, and we needed to purchase food and a few other personal items. In addition to the other items I purchased, I picked up some bleach and other cleaning supplies to be able to decontaminate our home once my son and I returned.

Once we left the store, Theresa suggested that we make a drive to my house, since we didn't encounter any water on the way to the store. She assured me that she would turn around if we came across any spots in the road that appeared to be flooded. I agreed to go with her, although I was fearful of encountering flooded areas where the water had not receded.

I said a prayer of protection over us so that Theresa could

navigate her way to drive to my house safely, because there were still high-level water spots all around the city of Houston. The news had cautioned everyone to stay inside if at all possible. It was as if Jesus literally took the wheel and drove my friend's SUV for her. She told me that the Holy Spirit guided her, as she intuitively knew when to get on the freeway to avoid the floodwater that was on the frontage roads, and just when to exit it where it was safe to drive through. The scarcely populated freeways looked as if the rapture had taken place. Cars were left abandoned on the side of the freeways, frontage roads, and in the fields beyond the frontage roads. They were positioned in the most ununiformed ways, as a result of their drivers unable to detect just how deep the floodwater really was until it was too late. As a result, their vehicles stalled out and failed them.

As we passed each abandoned vehicle, I wondered about the story behind each one, whether the drivers and their passengers survived and were all brought to safety. I prayed for a hopeful ending to their story.

There was such an eerie feeling as we turned onto FM517 in Dickinson. Theresa had to maneuver around the abandoned vehicles that were left in the middle of the street. There was such an unusually eerie quietness on my street. The usual sound of children playing and laughing was silenced by their absence, along with the constant barking of my next-door neighbor's dogs. The birds seemed to have had a moment of silence as well, and ceased to sing.

Theresa didn't go into the house with me, as I needed time alone to deal with my raw emotions once I saw all that was lost as a result of the flooding. Upon entering my home, the scent of an old and damp molded cellar hit my nostrils.

The floors were still saturated with remnants of the floodwater, but most of it had diminished. Parts of the wood flooring had settled out of place. Before my son and I had left our flooded home to be rescued, we'd already observed the damage to our wood flooring as it dismantled and floated from the water that rushed in.

The news had reported that the bacteria level was so high in the floodwater, that if you tried to salvage anything in your home that it touched, you were taking a serious health risk. Therefore, I had to get rid of all of my furniture downstairs.

I was grateful that all of our bedrooms were upstairs, so we didn't lose any of our bedroom furniture. Neither did we lose any of our clothing. All of our pictures were safely packed away upstairs too, because we had only moved there two months prior to the storm, and I didn't have the time to hang them up. That definitely worked out in our favor.

When I opened up the freezer, the food inside of it was thawed, and the food inside of the refrigerator was lukewarm due to its failed motor. So I had to replace it, too.

I dreaded opening the kitchen door that led into my garage. I hoped that there was still life left in my car since I had just paid it off the previous month. I wanted to avoid getting into another car loan for a while. I made my way into the garage, opened the car door and touched the carpet. To my surprise it was bone dry, which was puzzling because the waterline on the garage's wall clearly showed that water should have gotten in. Hopeful that the car would start, I stuck the key in the ignition. My engine immediately revved up loud and strong. That sound caused me to break down and cry tears of joy while I thanked God that He miraculously spared my car.

I had lost a lot in the past few months, and I guess God decided to have mercy on me by not allowing me to lose my car. There's no way to explain how it didn't flood, other than it was indeed a miracle.

I tried using the remote in the car to open the garage door, but it wouldn't budge. I left the car running and got out and went to the garage opener that was on the wall and I pressed it once. Only the sound of buzzing could be heard as the garage door struggled to release. I held it down for a while and it finally opened all the way up. Theresa stood outside of her car when she heard my engine start. She anxiously waited for me to back my car out of the garage and into the driveway.

We both praised God in the driveway, and then embraced each other as tears of joy ran from our eyes. I was hopeful that God had done the same for my son's car but I couldn't check since his keys were with him at Theresa's house.

Theresa said that she would trail behind me in her vehicle, just in case I encountered car troubles along the way. My car seemed a little slower than normal, but I made it all the way back to her house with no complications.

Theresa went into her house first and told her son and my son to help bring the Walmart bags in. They were both surprised to see my car.

My son had this great big smile on his face and said, "Maybe my car made it too!" Even though we were sitting on top of his car when we were rescued, he gained hope by seeing that my car didn't flood. I always told him that nothing was impossible, if he believed.

"Let's keep the faith believing that it did," I told him.

After we'd gotten our things inside, Tyquon and I headed

home. We pulled into our drive way and he got out to see if his car had survived the flooding. He opened his car door, then quickly turned his head away from the car and frowned, as the smell of mildew slapped him in the face. The floodwater lingered in his cup holders, and onto the cushions of his seats and the floors of his car.

He wanted to attempt to start the car so that he could let down the windows to air it out. He was so hopeful that it would start up just as mine did. When he turned the key in the ignition, not a sound escaped from the engine. He tried a few times but it continued to hold its peace and not make a sound. Up until that point, Tyquon had not shown his frustration and disappointment from the time the whole ordeal first began.

"It's going to be okay," I told him. "You'll get another car. I will make sure of that. That's what we have insurance for. You're just going to have to be patient because everyone will be filing claims. It's going to take time to get it all resolved. But you can rest assure that I will get you another car, Son."

Tyquon looked at me and said, "Yes, Mom," as the look of disappointment slowly eased off of his face.

After we brought our belongings in, I immediately called my landlord to let them know that their property was flooded. They said that they would send a construction crew out the next day to cut out the sheetrock and treat the walls to prevent the mold from growing.

I meditated on this: *That mold grows the most when it's covered up, in the dampest and darkest of places. The only way to get rid of it before it spread everywhere and contaminates your lungs, is to remove what it's hiding behind by cutting out what it is attached to, and then start over.*

I constantly tried to cover the mold that had been growing in my marriage from the beginning. Clayton only liked the idea of having a wife to hide behind, for his own convenience. His actions proved that his love was scarce, or if he had any at all for me. How long did he expect me to go on like this? Clayton wanted to show signs of affection in public places only. He held my hand while we were in church. He'd stick his chest out as he paraded me around different places we went, acting as if he was the proud husband. But once we returned home, he neglected me in every way. I contemplated over and over again, to remove myself from the situation temporarily, long enough to prompt Clayton to clean up the mold in his heart against me.

At the time however, I firmly believed that as a woman of faith, I could not walk away from Clayton. *If I walk away from him, what would people say, or think about me?* I'd often ponder on that very question while in my quite times. I was a prayer warrior. I wasn't supposed to run from the devil—the devil was supposed to run from me. However, the devil that I contended with in Clayton, had begun to put a good beating on me. In addition to the thoughts of disappointing people if I decided to leave Clayton, I battled within myself because I yet believed that God gave me Clayton as a result of my prayers. I went on numerous fasts for God to change my husband's heart toward me, but it never worked. It felt as if all of my fasting and praying was in vain. Although, looking back, God was only building me spiritually to be able to handle the reality of my situation when everything finally came to a head.

God was covering my son and me from the enemy that

lodged right under my roof. Had I not prayed so hard, I could have lost my mind in that hostile environment. I held on to the Word of God, through the darkest and lowest of valleys that I crawled my way through. His word alone gave me strength when I felt like throwing my hands up in defeat, instead I lifted them up in surrender to Him.

I began to see a steady and consistent flow in my clientele at the salon. My clientele began to stabilize within six months of starting to rebuild it in Houston. This was a great burden lifted off me as my income alone was able to sustain the needs of our entire household. I was so grateful when it did because I was so tired of hearing Clayton complain about paying a portion of the monthly bills. He wouldn't hesitate to call his parents at the first of every month to ask them for help. Before my clientele stabilized that December, I suggested to Clayton that we'd get a joint checking account to make weekly deposits, so that by the time the first of the month came around, we'd have the money to pay all of our bills. Clayton rejected my suggestion because at the time, I wasn't making the money that he was use to me making.

Clayton was so manipulative that once he saw the significant increase in my income he told me, "The Lord told me to tell you to add my name to your bank account. He said if you obey, He would fix the intimacy issues in our marriage."

I rolled my eyes at his suggestion. My son and I would have been living under a bridge and looking for our next meal, had I been stupid enough to listen to Clayton. I had tolerated a whole lot of mistreatment from him, and knew that he was getting over on me tremendously. But I was only doing what was necessary to maintain my household in order to take care of my son. Clayton just happened to be around to reap the benefits of it.

Clayton lied on the Lord, by using one of the things he knew I longed for in our marriage, intimacy, as a way to control and manipulate me into doing what he wanted me to do. He was coldblooded and definitely acting like the devil's advocate or his nearest of kin.

There is a saying, "What's done in the dark will come to the light." Clayton continued his behavior of staying out late in Houston, just as he had done in our hometown. He could no longer use the same excuses, so he stopped bothering to give me any.

Clayton would never let me know what his ever-changing work schedule was. When I was coming in from work, he would leave to avoid the constant agitation that my very presence seemed to bring him.

After my hours increased at the salon, I enrolled my son into an after-school karate program that he absolutely loved. I had to leave my clients at the salon to pick him up for 6:30pm on the nights I worked late. Most of my clients didn't know that I was married because I had little to no help from Clayton. Every now and then he would pick up my son when I asked him to, but that wasn't too often.

One day, I got Clayton to pick Tyquon up from his afterschool karate program. He got him something to eat, dropped him off at home, and then left. When I came home, I was upset that Clayton didn't tell me he was leaving out that night, or I would've had him drop my son off with me at the salon.

It was well past Tyquon's bedtime, so I made him get ready for bed. I was exhausted and went to bed, too. As soon as my head touched the pillow, the telephone rang.

"You have a collect call from Harris County Jail," the automated voice said.

My heart skipped a few beats as I accepted the call.

My husband's voice filled the phone. "Ruby, I've been arrested. The devil…."

I tuned him out. I was so tired of Clayton blaming all of his mishaps on "the devil." I wanted scream at him, "The devil cannot come after you, if you're riding along with him." I was fed up with all the drama that Clayton brought into our lives.

Although I was tired, I still tried to post Clayton's bail that night, but we weren't residents of Houston long enough, so I had to find a homeowner to cosign to post his bail. We lived in Houston under a year, so in order to assure the authorities that Clayton wouldn't skip town before his court date, a lien would be placed on the cosigner's home had he not shown up for court. I didn't know who to call that would commit themselves to such a burden without us living in Houston that long. I had one person in mind, Sadie.

Sadie was a Christian woman, married with two sons. Her younger son was the same age as mine. Sadie would pick up Tyquon from the salon on some Saturdays while I worked, and took him to play with her son. She was God-sent. She never judged me after I decided to open up to her about my marriage. She'd patiently listen to me as I cried, trying to figure out how I could make things work with Clayton. She'd give me such words of comfort, then she'd suggest that I stopped doing her hair for a moment to pray with me. I knew that I could confide in her about anything.

CHAPTER SIXTEEN

I picked up my phone and called Sadie.

"Hey Baby," she answered on the first ring. "How are you?"

The second I heard Sadie's voice, I had an emotional meltdown. I spilled out the details of Clayton's arrest. I was talking so fast while crying, that it was hard for her to understand me.

"Slow down, Baby. What do you need me to do to help you?" she said.

I calmed myself down so that I could clearly tell her what was going on.

"Clayton was arrested late last night. I tried to go down there to bail him out, but we haven't been living here long enough to post his bail without a cosigner. They said that I had to find a homeowner who's been living here for more than a year, in order for me to post his bail. Only if Clayton didn't show up for his court date, would any responsibility fall on the cosigner. And trust me when I say, he will be there."

Sadie paused for a moment and then said, "Ruby, I am

only doing this for you, because I don't know your husband. Let me know where I need to meet you, and what you need me to do."

I was overcome with emotions again. "Thank you so much! I owe you my life."

"Just know that I'm only doing this for you," she reiterated. "Do you need any help with the bail?"

I declined her offer. "You agreeing to cosigner is more than enough. "I promise that you don't have to worry about him not appearing in court. Trust me, he will be there," I said.

Sadie replied, "I surely hope so."

It took a few hours to process Clayton out of jail. When he finally did, he looked totally exhausted and famished. The minute our eyes met, tears ran down both of our faces.

I tried to explain my delay. "Clayton, I'm sorry, I tried to bail you out last night but they wouldn't let me. The bail bondsman required you to have a cosigner, a homeowner that's been a resident for more than a year. I had to ask one of my clients to be a cosigner, and that's what took so long. But if it wasn't for her, you would still be in there."

More tears welled up in his eyes and he said, "I'm so embarrassed that you had to get one of your clients involved. I don't want you to lose out on any business on my behalf. Make sure you tell her that I said thank you, because she did not have to do that." Clayton paused. "Does Ty know that I was arrested?"

I nodded. "Yes, I had no choice in telling him because I had to wake him up and take him with me last night when I tried to post your bail. He kept asking where were we going."

Clayton said, "I am really so embarrassed. I'm supposed

to be an example to him. I've never been arrested in my life. Can you believe the cops decided to mess with me now? When I was out there gangbanging and selling drugs, they couldn't find me."

"Clayton, what exactly happened? Why did they arrest you?"

He shrugged. "I really don't know why they arrested me. I was on my way to the church, to meet one of the ministers for the church's business meeting. Some panhandler asked me for some money. As I was stopped to give him change, the cops pulled up behind me and told me to get out of the car. This cop threw me down on the ground and handcuffed me, then threw me in the back of his cruiser. I didn't know that it was a crime to give out change."

"Well, if you only were giving change to a homeless person, do you think that you were racially profiled?"

"No. The officer was a minority, too."

I drove in silence the rest of the way home, trying to rationalize Clayton's story. It sounded like a whole chunk of the story was missing. They had charged him with probable cause and evading arrest. Therefore, I had the great task of finding an attorney to represent Clayton, in order to clear his name of the charges. I had hopes of Clayton finding better employment, and a felony on his record would have completely wipe out those dreams.

The drama seemed to never end. Just when I felt my nose breaking through the threshold of the water's surface to inhale the air above me, something always seemed to grab my legs below, leaving me fighting to come up for air once again. I had just begun to get back on my feet financially. I didn't know how I would manage all of the bills, on top of paying a lawyer to clear Clayton's name.

At dinner, my son ate his food and his eyes began to get heavy at the table from the long night we had. I made him go take a shower, and he was fast asleep before his head was able to sink into the pillow good.

I got into the bathtub, reclined my head, and submerged my body underneath the water. I closed my eyes and prayed for guidance on finding a good lawyer, although I wasn't totally clear on what we were up against. I was truly exhausted with my marriage, and I was especially tired of fighting for it by myself.

At the time of Clayton's arrest, the last time he made love to me was when we lived in Massachusetts. I flat-out stopped wearing my sexy negligee to bed, so when I got out of the bathtub, I put on my cotton nightie. I crawled onto my side of the bed and beat Clayton to the punch, turning my back on him, so that he wouldn't have to bother turning his back on me. I pulled the covers over my body, and closed my eyes to go to sleep. I was awakened by tender kisses on the back of my neck. My husband's hands massaged my bosom as his nature knocked on the back of my thighs, anxiously waiting for access.

My thoughts were: *I must be dreaming.*

Clayton turned me over, hovered over me and kissed my lips passionately. All my exhaustion disappeared and I was fully awakened in every way.

"Ruby, I love you." Clayton chanted those words over and over, as he kissed my ears, neck and various parts of my body.

"I love you too, Honey," I moaned as the feeling of ecstasy swallowed me up.

There wasn't a part of my body that my husband left unkissed. Making love to me that night was Clayton's way of showing gratitude for me coming to his rescue. Or perhaps, it was his way of making a down payment, to ensure him that I would be with him all the way. Until I exhausted all of my energy and funds into clearing his name of the pending charges that were against him.

Making love should be part of being married, but Clayton seemed to have used it as an annual incentive to keep me hanging on to the hope of a positive change. Which in essence was his way to manipulate me. However, I wanted to savor the moment of being intertwined in passionate love-making. In that moment, I didn't care what his motives were. I was completely lost in the intoxication of his love. Clayton knew just how to hit all of the right spots. The sad part about it was, I just didn't know when he would decide to hit them all again.

Clayton exerted all of his energy into pleasing me, then collapsed on my chest. I held his head and kissed the top of it, not wanting to let it go. As I caressed his head, I prayed that God would completely transform his mind and his heart toward me, and make him the man that He called him to be.

Clayton lifted up his head and said, "What are you doing?"

"Oh nothing," I replied. "Just said a little prayer for you."

Clayton got up out of the bed, threw on his robe, and left the room. His moods would often switch as fast as lightning, so I wasn't sure if I turned the switch on without knowing it. He came back in with a drink and he guzzled it down as he stood in front of the bed. Clayton extended the cup toward me, so that I could rehydrate after the highly intense workout we had.

I took a sip, then handed the cup back to him and he turned it up until it was empty, then placed it onto the night stand. Clayton crawled back into the bed and wrapped his arms tightly around me, pulling me in so close, that his chest became my pillow.

"Honey, thank you for praying for me. I'm going to need all of your prayers and support, to help get me through this."

Clayton used the same old line, every time he was getting ready to ask me for something.

"You have to remember, Ruby, that it was your prayers that brought us together in the first place, and if it brought us together it's going to take them to keep us together. So Baby, please don't stop praying for me," he said.

"I won't, Honey," I replied. "I won't stop praying for you."

"Well, Baby, you know that I want to find better employment so that I could take care of our household. But first, I'm going to need to be totally exonerated of the pending charges against me, to be able to do it."

And there it was. All of a sudden, Clayton wanted to convince me that he was desperately in search of a better job prior to his arrest. He continued to lie about his "job search" claiming it came to a screeching halt after his arrest.

"No one wants to hire me with these charges hanging over my head," he sounded sincere at times. But the truth was, he never looked for a better job before he was arrested.

Clayton gave me a false sense of hope. He knew that I had become quite exhausted with carrying the entirety of our household financially. So he pretended that he would give me some financial relief when he found a better job, after I cleared his name.

Clayton was in denial of just how dysfunctional our marriage really was. The number one lesson I learned from that was, God will not force a person against their freewill to love anyone, no matter how much you love that person and desire their love in return. There has to be mutual and genuine love between both parties for a marriage to survive. Clayton would tell me that he loved me numerous times, and on different occasions throughout our seven-year marriage, but his actions didn't prove it. I was willing to hang on to empty promises that were proven to be falsehood, without the power of action deeming them as truth.

CHAPTER SEVENTEEN

The district court kept on resetting Clayton's case. It was finally brought to trial almost a year after his arrest. I knew that he faced charges of probable cause and evading arrest. However, I wasn't aware of all the details until it was revealed at his trial.

The trial had finally come. I fasted and prayed the entire week leading up to it, so that God would intervene, and the charges would be dropped.

"Honey, it's going to be okay," I told him as we pulled up to the courthouse. "God has us, and He let me know in prayer, that everything is going to be all right and the charges will be dropped."

Clayton became overwhelmed with emotion, as we sat in the car in front of the courthouse.

"I really hope so," he said. "I just want this to be all behind us so that we can move on with our lives."

"You just have to keep the faith, and believe that it's already done," I told him.

We got out of the car and walked hand-in-hand up the stairs of the court as a united front. Our lawyer was waiting for us at the top of the stairs and we followed him into the courtroom. Clayton and I continued to hold hands all the way into the courtroom until we took our seats. I took my seat two rows behind where Clayton and his lawyer were seated. Clayton sat down and turned around to look back at me, with a nervous smile on his face.

When the prosecution began to unfold their case against Clayton, I felt as though my spirit had leaped out of my body and I almost fell from my seat. The prosecution said that Clayton was parked illegally in the middle of a street that was high in male prostitution. They said that Clayton had his window down talking to a man, and when the police pulled up behind him to question him about the situation, he evaded arrest.

Out of all things that the probable cause charge could have been, I was not expecting to hear that the police who arrested Clayton that night, thought that he was soliciting a male prostitute. In Clayton's defense, our lawyer presented him as a loving husband with a child, and a man of the cloth, who had no prior charges before he was arrested. I sat there in shock, and screamed within myself thinking, *This man touches me only once a year, and I had my son before I met him.* However, I held my peace and held myself together on the outside, despite my inner turmoil.

There was a fifteen-minute recess and I met Clayton and the lawyer in the hallway. Clayton was livid at the picture that the prosecution had painted of him.

"Can you believe them?" he barked. "I wouldn't have to go all the way downtown to find a male prostitute."

The lawyer frowned, then corrected him. "You mean you wouldn't go *anywhere* to find a male prostitute, because you have a wife and a child, and that would put her in danger… and furthermore, you don't indulge in that type of behavior as a minister."

Clayton just stood there in silence until the attorney motioned for us to go back into the courtroom. It didn't take long for a jury return a 'not guilty' verdict. Clayton was ecstatic. He threw his arms around me, but I didn't match his joy. I had an uneasy feeling in my stomach. I thought of all of the times Clayton rejected me, all the excuses, especially the last one.

Just months before his trial, Clayton had convinced me that he found a place called the Get Well Clinic. He claimed it was located in the Texas Medical Center. He had been faithfully going twice a week to get treatment for impotence.

Once, I asked how the treatments were going.

He answered with an attitude, "This takes time, don't expect any changes overnight. The doctor said it's one of the most severe cases that he has ever treated. He told me I need to minimize my stress levels so that the treatments could have full effect. Asking questions about it only puts pressure and stress on me, and I will not get better if you keep on pressuring me."

One night, when I was up late watching television, an infomercial came on, with the same name as the place Clayton was going to get treated for his impotence. I called the number provided on the television screen, to get more information to see just how long it would take before the treatment would start to work on him.

"Hello. Is your clinic located in the Texas Medical Center?" I asked.

"Oh, ma'am. We're not a clinic," the person on the other

end of the phone said. "This is just a series of CD's that you can purchase if you are depressed."

When I confronted Clayton about it, he blew up and left the house, and never mentioned the "Get Well" clinic again.

I pushed aside that memory as Clayton navigated the car home. I felt him looking at me. Then finally, he said, "Ruby, I know you may be thinking there's some truth to what the prosecution said because there's been little intimacy in our marriage."

I interjected, "Clayton, that's an understatement. You only make love to me once a year."

Clayton said, "Yeah, I know it's been rough, but it's not what it appears to be. It's not true what you've heard in the courtroom today, so put your mind at ease. The devil always wanted to paint this bad picture of me, Ruby. I can't believe that the same spirit that tried to tarnish my name in Springfield, followed me to Houston. I'm so tired of the devil. Ruby, you have to believe that I am not indulging in that type of behavior. I love you. Do you really think that I would bring you all the way down here, so that I could deceive you and live a double life?"

"Clayton, I want to believe you, and continue to believe *in* you, but you've given me absolutely nothing to stand on but grief," I cried.

Clayton replied, "You have to believe me, Ruby. Being stressed-out has played a major role in my lack of desire to be intimate with you. I haven't been making the money that I should to provide for you and Tyquon. But I promise you that it's going to get better now that my name is cleared. Baby, please trust me when I say it's going to get better."

I held my peace.

Clayton continued to plead his case to me like I was the prosecutor who'd cross examined him. "Maybe this happened to get my attention, so that I could appreciate all that God has blessed me with." Clayton even threw in a church cliché when he said, "I've been focusing on all my problems and not the problem solver. Ruby, you've been right by my side through all of the madness that I've been going through, and put you through, too. I'm just counting my blessings to have a praying woman. I don't know what the outcome of all of this would have been, had you not fasted and prayed for me. I would be a fool to let you go."

Clayton released one of his hands from the steering wheel, and held my hand. He would periodically take his eyes off of the road to glance over me with a smile on his face. It appeared as if the blinders came off Clayton's eyes, and he saw me as the wife that stood before him at the altar when he sang his heart out to me on the day we committed our lives to one another. So, I decided to believe my husband, and continue to hope that things would change for the better as he promised it would. I know he sounded like a broken record, but I chose to put my faith in him and God.

Spring had come, and it was finally time to do some Spring cleaning. I had come to the end of my rope battling with the same issues in my marriage. Clayton's name had been cleared, but very little had changed, except he moved from the women's shoe department on the first floor, up to selling furniture on the second floor. He said that selling furniture would allow him to make more money.

But when I asked him to help me pay the bills, he said, "No one is coming to buy furniture at Macy's."

At various times, Clayton would show me his check stubs, which were very low. Some amounted to two hundred dollars or less. So I simply stopped asking him to help out with the bills. And just when I thought that my marriage was at its lowest, the drill of Clayton's hatred for me pushed it further into the ground. I was in the biggest spiritual battle of my life.

Not long after the trial, Clayton tried to prove to me that he was indeed, a man of God, and not the person the prosecution made him out to be. He wanted me to believe that he was a prophet—that his words came straight out of the mouth of God.

"Mark my words. Everyone who's lied about my sexual preference is going to die, including your family," he barked.

Clayton swore that my family was spreading rumors in our hometown of the intimacy issues we had in our marriage, but it wasn't true. I never discussed our intimacy issues with my family, nor the probable cause theory of the trial. I believe that "death and life are in the power of the tongue" (Prov. 18:21). Therefore, I had to pray against the spoken curses of death, that Clayton spewed out of his mouth against my mother and sisters. Clayton seemed to be getting too spiritually deep - to the point of insanity.

One night, Clayton woke up and jumped out of the bed, and started to repeat the same words, "There's a spirit of deception all over this place" as he paced the floor in anger.

After a while, I couldn't take it anymore and said, "Clayton, what are you talking about?"

"Oh, everybody loves Ruby, they think you're such an innocent angel. You got everybody else fooled, but I can see straight through you. I can see that deceptive spirit in you."

By this time, I was fed up with Clayton's strange behavior and interrupted his crazy rant. "Clayton, what exactly are you talking about?"

"The Lord told me that you're cheating on me with the drummer at church. I'm not having sex with you, so you're getting it from him," he yelled.

That was one, out of the umpteenth times, that Clayton accused me of infidelity with random people. He paced as he kept mumbling. "I couldn't understand why God took the desire away from me to be with you intimately. And then God spoke to me. He told me you've been committing adultery. God has been protecting me, His prophet, from such filth."

I stared at him in disbelief. "I've been faithful to you, Clayton! Are you purposely withholding sex from me to provoke me into cheating on you?" I asked. "If you want to leave me, you don't have to create a story to do it…just leave!"

I had just about enough of Clayton's world of insanity. I was ready to walk through the exit door of our marriage.

Clayton grabbed some of his belongings and crammed them into a couple of trash bags. It seemed as though he had intentions of not coming back for a while. He looked back at me one last time before he stormed out of the door.

I was still sitting there, stunned a few hours later when he returned. He had a pitiful look on his face and tears in his eyes.

"The Lord said if I leave now, then the devil will get the victory over our marriage," he said. "We can't let the devil win."

I was tired. And I wondered if my love was enough to

keep me on the emotional rollercoaster ride, that my marriage had been on from the very beginning. I thought of an exit plan. We were six years into our marriage, and he was the only one who reaped the benefits of our so-called union. I knew the time had come to love myself more than I loved him.

The next day, I headed over to the Skylar Pointe Apartment complex. I walked into the front office to inquire about their two-bedroom apartments. There was one that met my budget with just enough space for my son and me to start our lives over. After filling out the application, I paid a three-hundred-dollar application fee. I had to wait for them to call me back after they did a criminal back ground check, and to see if my credit was approved. The leasing office called me a few days later, and I was scheduled to move the following month.

I didn't say a word to anyone about my plans to leave Clayton. However, it was as if Clayton had sensed that his time with me was coming to an end, because he wanted to plan a getaway for the weekend. He wanted to take me to the Galleria and stay overnight at one of the hotels in the area.

"I want to tell you how sorry I am. I really hope and pray that we can start our marriage over," he said.

I'll admit that his pleading was getting to me. And I began to questioned my decision to leave Clayton. I wanted to make sure that I wasn't making the decision to leave him based off of sheer exhaustion and frustration with my situation. I wanted to be sure that God was really speaking to my heart to leave Clayton. I wrestled with the idea that God was not particularly in favor of divorce. But I had to keep telling myself that God wasn't in favor of me living miserably either, with someone who refused to change or love me.

As ridiculous as it sounds, I decided to give Clayton one last chance before I separated from him for good. I knew at this point that it would take a miracle, but I was hopeful that nothing was impossible for God.

The night we headed to the hotel, I walked out with my overnight bag in my hand. Clayton grabbed my bag.

"I don't want you to lift a finger to do a thing. I got it, Honey."

When we got into the car, Clayton put in a CD of R&B slow jams and turned the volume down low, as he talked to me in a soft and romantic tone.

"Baby, I know that our marriage has been very rocky, but I don't want to lose you. Besides Jesus, you are the best thing that's ever happened to me," he said.

I didn't respond as we continued to the Westheimer area. We pulled into the parking lot of the Quality Inn. While some might've turned their nose up at that, I wasn't looking to be brought to a five-star hotel. I wanted to see my husband earnestly put forth an effort to work on our broken marriage.

We put our stuff in the room, then left to grab a bite to eat. We stopped at an inexpensive pub that Clayton said had the best sandwiches. One thing I had observed that night, was Clayton knew how to dine on a budget, when he was responsible for paying the bill.

After we ate, Clayton said, "Honey, let's go back to the room. I'm ready for you. I just have to stop at CVS to pick up a couple of things."

We headed to CVS, where Clayton picked up a couple of Red Bulls, some water, and a pack of condoms. Once we made it back to the hotel, Clayton showered first and then I took my shower immediately after, bringing my night bag in the bathroom with me.

I walked back in the bedroom with tempered excitement. My heart dropped when I saw Clayton on the bed – asleep.

"It's your own fault," I mumbled as I climbed in the bed next to him and envisioned how I'd move all my belongings out.

I woke up to Clayton saying, "No, this night is not about to go down like this. Ruby, what time is it?"

I shook off my sleep as I looked over at my phone. "It's almost three in the morning."

Clayton leaned over and kissed me. "Honey, I'm sorry, I'm about to get up." Clayton jumped out of the bed, went to the refrigerator, opened one of the Red Bulls and guzzled it down without taking a breath.

He went into the restroom and when he came out, he seemed to have gotten his wings, full of energy and ready to make love to me. Clayton climbed into the bed and pulled the covers off me.

"Honey, you look so good. You got that just for me?"

"Yes, this is all for you," I said.

Clayton laid on top of me while we kissed passionately. We rolled over and switched positions as we kissed and caressed one another some more. Clayton pulled off my lingerie and put on a condom.

"I want you to lay back and enjoy the ride," Clayton moaned as his kisses trailed south.

I grabbed the pillow and bit down on it, so my joyful sound wouldn't be heard in the next room. I grabbed the top of Clayton's head, overcome by ecstasy, as he continued to eat of my love cuisine. My insides quaked and I could no longer hold my composure, as my love cup filled to capacity.

My love overflowed like the honey from a honeycomb, as I screamed out Clayton's name. Clayton came up for air, with the residue of honey all over his face. He slowly kissed his way up above my waist to my bosom. I obeyed Clayton and laid there, letting him do all of the pleasing.

Clayton looked into my eyes. "Are you ready for me?"

"Yes. Yes, I'm ready," I moaned.

Clayton entered the passageway of my body, to regain the control and influence that he'd lost over my mind and spirit. For intimacy is so much more than skin deep, it is spirit deep.

I took a deep breath as my heart seemed to skip a few beats. He reacquainted himself with my inner parts. He went in over and over again, and refused to let up until my love continued to pour out. It washed away all thoughts of me leaving him. He pounded his love into me until I couldn't fathom the thought of walking away from him without giving it another try. He went in more intensely and nonstop, as he asked me the question "Do you love me, Honey?"

"Yes, I love you!" I screamed.

"Then please don't leave me."

Clayton asked me the same question, and received the same response from me, until he no longer could hold back the flow of his love. He laid on top of me covered in sweat.

I stroked the back of Clayton's head and then kissed the top of it as he laid there exhausted on my chest. My hands caressed and massaged him, then traced the outline of his well-defined back. I laid there and wondered how Clayton found out that I planned on leaving him.

Whatever the case, Clayton had me back in his love trance. I was back under his spell and hopeful once again for a positive change in my marriage. After our overnight getaway that weekend, we both signed a year's lease to stay at our current apartment. I called Skylar Pointe Apartment's leasing office, to tell them that I no longer needed the apartment. However, the application fee was nonrefundable.

CHAPTER EIGHTEEN

Unfulfilled promises, false hopes, and shattered dreams were never the reality of what I thought my life would turn out to be. I had envisioned a glorious life when I had given my life to Christ. I pictured living life as if it were pure gold, and far from the insanity that my days turned out to be, when I made the commitment and said, "Yes" to Jesus.

I'll live for You…I'll follow You, wherever You want me to go. I didn't know I would have to follow You through the trenches in the lowest of valleys, and through the murkiest of waters in the mysterious deep green sea. I never envisioned that I would have to contend against that great dragon of the sea. Struggling to come up for air, all while vigorously trying to avoid the fire that came out of his nostrils against me. So, I held up the shield of faith, knowing it would quench all the fiery darts of the wicked that threatened to end my life.

Even with the reality of the doom that tries to captivate my soul…even through the dragged out overextended tribulation that constantly taunts my mind to turn around and say, "NO." There's a faith that resides deep within me, that continues to tell me to take a stand and still say, "Yes to

You."

I did not know if I could spend another minute living with Clayton, let alone another year.

Immediately after I signed another lease at the apartment with Clayton, his horns appeared once again, but even more pronounced. The getaway was a guise. The only thing that Clayton wanted to save was the roof over his head.

Clayton stopped going to church altogether. I knew that was a trick of the enemy so that he wouldn't hear the Word. Which only made the horrible matters we were dealing with in our marriage more disastrous. Clayton continued to want everyone to see him as this great man of God. All I wanted him to be was a good husband to me, and a better stepfather to my son. Clayton went off on one of his "prophetic" rants again.

"Everybody is going to have to look up at me when God elevates me," he cried. "I'm not just an average man, the world will see that God speaks to me. People are about to start dropping like flies, when they put their mouths on me."

Clayton's craziness was taking a huge toll on me. Depression was trying to take hold of my mind, and although I got out of the bed every day to take care of my son and go to work, it had truly become a struggle. I needed to feel the reassurance of the people who I knew genuinely loved me, and had my back. So, I planned a trip home to be around my mother and sisters. I wanted all of us to go so Clayton could see his family, too.

"Ruby, I think it's a great idea for you and Ty to visit home, but without me," Clayton said. "You need to take a break because you've been working so hard, after paying off the lawyer for me, and carrying the weight of all of the bills.

If I go, that would be another expense. That money could be used for you and Ty to enjoy the trip. I'll just stay home."

Although I needed a break from Clayton, his suggestion didn't sit well with me. I didn't trust him staying behind, and I felt he had something up his sleeve for after my son and I left town. "I really think it would be good that you come, too. I don't want to leave you behind. You need a getaway to relieve your mind from the stress of that arrest."

"Trust me, you need this trip more than I need it. I'll be here waiting for you when you get back," he insisted.

I decided not to fight him on it and called my sister, Gail, so that she could book two round-trip airline tickets for my son and me, since she was such an expert at finding them at discounted rates.

Gail was so excited. "Just tell me the dates to book and I'll immediately start looking for three tickets. After I find them, I'll give you a call back to get your credit card information. I can't wait to see you all."

"You'll only have to look for tickets for me and Ty because Clayton is not coming with us."

Gail said, "He's not? I would've loved to have seen him, too."

"Yes, I know. He decided to stay home to cut down the cost of the trip. He said the money that I would have spent on his ticket could go toward our spending money."

"That is so thoughtful of him to send the two of you home without him."

My sister was unaware of all the money I had to spend on Clayton to clear his name, and the fact that he wasn't contributing to our trip home, or anything else concerning us for that matter.

Gail quickly found two round-trip tickets for me and my son to visit in three weeks. In addition to booking the trip for me, she asked if I would be willing to speak at the church for one of the programs they were having the week I was visiting. I wanted to tell her that I was the one who needed to be ministered to with all the turmoil I had endured. However, I never turned down an opportunity to be used by God, no matter how low I was feeling, so I agreed.

I went on a twenty-one day fast leading up to my trip home. I needed a supernatural and divine power to fight the battle I felt powerless to fight alone. I laid on the couch on my day off, after I saw my son off to school. I was barely able to muster up the strength to get up to do the things I needed to do around the house. I had to get a song in my heart, like my mother had in her heart years ago, when she was going through hell with my abusive father. Although I felt like laying down permanently, I had so much to live for. If my mother didn't lay down and die with all of the adversity that she had to face with five of us to care for, I knew that I could live through all my mine.

I began to sing. *"Because He Lives I can face tomorrow. Because He Lives all of my fears are gone…My life is worth living because He lives."*

I continued to sing and pray while I did things around the house, and the clouds of depression slowly began to lift. After I prepared dinner, I began to prepare the message I was going to give when I went home to visit. The message that God dropped in my spirit was *"This Place Is Not My Final Destination"* and for a subtopic, *"I Have a Hopeful Future."* The text came from Jeremiah 29:11, "For I know the plans I have for you, plans to prosper you and not to harm you, to give you a hope and a future." This was a message of hope to me and all of those who were listening, who'd experienced the squeeze of life's seemingly endless difficulties and hardships. That difficult place may seemed to have made a permanent place of residency in one's life but, it's only temporary.

When the time came for our trip, my son was so excited because we hadn't been home in three years. As we gathered our suitcases to get ready to go to the airport, Clayton put on the performance of his life. He had an exaggerated sad face, as if he couldn't bear to see us leaving him behind.

"Oh, Clayton, cut it out. I tried to tell you to come with us. Now stop looking as if you're losing your best friend. I'll be back soon."

"I'm really going to miss both of you. I'm not going to know what to do with myself without you all being here."

"Don't throw any wild parties while I'm gone," I said.

Clayton laughed and said, "Now why would I throw a party? I'm just going to be working and coming home every day to work on my music while you're gone. Partying is going to be the furthest thing from my mind. I'm sorry that I can't bring you to the airport today, or pick you up when you come back. I hate that I have to work on both days."

Something definitely did not sit well in my spirit, but I was just ready to go. Clayton kissed me on my face and whispered in my ear, "I love you. I'll be waiting for you to get back home. Have a good trip."

I told Clayton, "I love you, too. I'll call you when we make it there."

Our flight had begun to gradually descend over Hartford, Connecticut. We encountered turbulence while breaking through the cloudy atmosphere. After we deplaned, I was on a mission to go directly to see my mother. I wanted to feel the warmth of her embrace, as it silently assured me that everything was all right.

My mother greeted us with excitement. "My babies are home!" We embraced and cried together, not wanting to let each other go. "Oh and look at my handsome grandson! Look at how big he's gotten," she said, as she hugged Tyquon tightly and kissed the top of his head.

"Grandma, I missed you," Ty said.

"I missed you so much, too!"

My oldest sister, Lakeisha, came from around the corner. She'd been going through dialysis, but seemed to gain strength and energy from seeing us. Her face lit up as I walked toward her to embrace her, and we both cried as we held on to one another. The drastic change in my sister's appearance had hit me hard as her diabetes and kidney failure had begun to take its toll on her body. It was an emotional but joyous reunion, as I embraced all four of my sisters, from the oldest down to the youngest. It was the first time in a long time, that all five of my mother's daughters were in the same room together. My mother wanted to capture the moment, and raised her voice to be heard beyond the loudness amongst us.

"It's not too often that we're all here together. I want to take a picture with all five of my babies."

Gail handed her camera to one of our nieces to take the picture. I didn't know the picture we took that day at Vanessa's apartment, would be the last picture taken of all of us together.

My son and I stayed with Vanessa since she had the extra room because she was separated from her husband at the time of my visit. My mother was living down the walkway with Lakeisha to help take care of her. So we would take turns spending nights between the both of their living quarters. It just felt so good to be in the presence of genuine family love.

Lakeisha had every last one of Tyler Perry's plays. When I stopped by her room, she was watching *"What's Done in the Dark."* Immediately after I heard them sing the lyrics to the theme song, *"What's done in the dark, will come to the light,"* I had an eerie feeling that God was about to reveal some things to me.

I tried calling Clayton before I went to bed, but he continued not to answer his phone. He hadn't answered earlier when I called either. I said a prayer for him and closed my eyes to go to sleep.

The following afternoon, I received a call from an unfamiliar number. When I picked it up, it was Clayton.

"Hello, Honey. I know that you were trying to call me, but I went to the rodeo with Max. You wouldn't believe what happened. I got on a ride, and my phone flew off and shattered in a thousand pieces."

Max was one of Clayton's musician friends that he had met a few months ago. He was supposed to be helping him make a gospel CD.

"The number I'm calling you from is a temporary number. I purchased a go-phone while my phone is being fixed. So make sure that you save this number."

I listened to Clayton, but his story didn't add up to me. I really didn't believe him, but I didn't question his story at the time. I knew my time with my family was limited, and I wasn't trying to waste time combing through Clayton's lies.

"Okay, Clayton. I'll save it right after we hang up."

"I know that God is going to use you greatly tonight. Don't hold back, Ruby. I love you."

"Thank you, Clayton. I love you, too."

I arrived at the church early enough to be able to greet church members, family and friends that I had not seen since I left my hometown. The love was overwhelming as everyone was so excited to see my son and me. Clayton's mother started the devotional service like she had always done when I was still attending their church. Nothing much had changed, and I was right at home. All of my sisters and family were there, and to my surprise my Bishop, Clayton's brother walked through the door to hear me speak, just before I took the podium.

Whenever it was time for me to take the podium to deliver a message, no matter how large or small the crowd was, I would get a nervous feeling down in the pit of my stomach. It wouldn't leave until the Spirit took over and began to calm my nerves.

God had His perfect way that night, and a lot of people came up for prayer after I delivered the message. I realized that I wasn't the only person who felt trapped, stuck, or sentenced to a *place* of various hardships and tribulations that needed a word of encouragement. It was a glorious night in the small Pentecostal church as God used me the way He saw fit. I could finally exhale, as the responsibility of delivering God's word, and the fast was now behind me.

I was ready to let my hair down, eat, and have some fun with my family. We planned a night of pizza and bowling with the entire family the next day. Lakeisha wasn't feeling well, but pushed herself to come out with the rest of us. She began to feel better as the excitement of all of us clowning around together, seemed to have given her strength. Surprisingly, Lakeisha gained enough strength and participated in a few of the bowling frames. My mother loved bowling and was very competitive with it. We'd all had a great time that night.

The next day, my son and I went to Clayton's parents' house to spend time with them, and so that my son could eat his favorite meatloaf recipe from Clayton's mother. Just when we were almost finished eating the delicious meal, their house phone rang. Clayton's father answered it in the other room, then called his wife away from the table to get on the phone.

Shortly thereafter, she came back upstairs to get me to take the phone call in the basement, so that no one else in the house could hear the conversation.

"Ruby, it's Clayton on the phone. He's been arrested again."

I was completely lost for words and became numb at that very moment. It just didn't make any sense to me. Clayton getting arrested while I was away had confirmed that he was up to no good. I didn't know the nature of his arrest, nor did I really care. I had already made up in my mind that I was not going to be as involved in his second arrest, as I was with his first.

His mother said, "Ruby, I'm so sorry that this happened again, and so soon. This is just too much."

Our flight was scheduled to leave the next day. It was an emotional farewell session we said good-bye to all of our loved ones at my mother's house. I embraced all of my sisters, but I held on to Lakeisha for a little longer. She cried just as bad as the day that I told her I was going to relocate to

Houston. My son and I put our suitcases into the rental car to head to the airport to catch our flight. The feeling of sadness engorged my very soul, being fully aware of the utter hell I had to face at home with Clayton. We boarded the plane and took our seats and headed back to Houston.

CHAPTER NINETEEN

My marriage was nothing but secrets, lies, and more deceit. It was hard for me to decipher and rationalize the truth, from the falsehood of deceit and endless lies that Clayton regurgitated.

It was the Monday after we returned from visiting my hometown, and almost a week from the day I picked my husband up from the county jail—for the second time. Although Clayton's mother had given me most of his bail money, I still had to pay for his car to get out of the police impound.

It was my day off from work. I sat on my living room sofa trying to make sense of the story Clayton told me of his arrest. He claimed he'd been sitting in his car at the park smoking a cigarette, when the police decided to harass him and take him to jail. I sat on the couch deep in thought about Clayton's second arrest and my plans to exit my marriage. My thoughts were interrupted by a knocking on the door. I looked outside, and it was Max. I thought he had possibly forgotten a piece of his equipment at our place.

"Hello, Max. How are you?" I said after I'd let him in.

"Hi, Ruby, I'm good. I'm sorry to disturb you, but I'm very concerned about Clayton. I haven't seen him for a while, and I've been trying to call him, but his phone kept going straight to voicemail."

My antenna immediately went up since Clayton had claimed they were working on his music the entire week I was gone. Not to mention the trip to the rodeo.

However, I refrained from saying anything. "I'll get Clayton out of the bedroom," I said. "Have a seat. Would you like anything to drink?"

"I'll have some water."

I went into the refrigerator and handed him a cold bottle of water, and went into the bedroom to get Clayton.

"You have a visitor."

"Who is it?"

"Clayton, just come out here and see."

Clayton came out of the bedroom and walked into the living room. When he saw it was Max, he appeared startled.

"H-Hey Max, what's going on?"

"I normally don't just pop up on people unannounced, but I was concerned about you. I've been calling your phone, but it's been going straight to voicemail."

I waited to see what excuse Clayton would make up to cover the lie he told me. He slowly sat down next to Max.

"Oh, my phone is being fixed now."

I wanted there to be no possible way that Clayton would try to wiggle his way out of this one.

I said, "Hey, Max, how was the rodeo?"

"The rodeo? I haven't been to the rodeo. I would like to go one day, though," Max replied.

Clayton sat looking stupid.

"Max, you *haven't* been to the rodeo this year?"

"No, I have never been. Why do you ask?" Max said.

"I was just asking, it's a real fun place. You should go and check it out one day," I answered.

Max said, "I think I will. Well, I don't want to disturb the two of you. I just stopped by to make sure that you were okay, Clayton."

"Yeah, uh, my phone should be coming through UPS, any day now," Clayton said, unable to look me in the eye.

"I really appreciate you stopping by to show your concern for Clayton. You're such a great friend," I said.

"That's what friends are for. You all enjoy the rest of your day."

After Max left, Clayton closed the door and returned to the same spot on the couch. I sat next to him and waited to see if he would voluntarily address the lie he told me. Clayton just sat there and didn't open his mouth as if nothing happened.

"So you worked on music with Max the entire week I was out of town, and broke your phone with him at the rodeo? Clayton, *really*?"

Clayton didn't open his mouth, he just stared straight ahead of him as if he were blind and mute.

"God told me that He was going to reveal some things to me," I continued. "Then boom, first the arrest, and then bam, here comes Max knocking on the door on my day off. Think about it, he could have come on a day that I was at work, but God had it be this way to expose your lies. Do you think that the Lord is going to keep allowing you to lie to me, and treat me the way you do? Do you *really* think that you can keep on mistreating me, and God wouldn't show me the person I'm really dealing with? How long do you think that you can play with God, and toy around with my heart and He not hold you accountable for your actions? Clayton, who were you *really* with?"

Clayton said, "Man, you're trippin.' I don't have to sit here and listen to this."

Clayton got up from the couch and went into the bedroom to grab his keys.

"Yeah, I must have struck a nerve. When a lie is told, it's usually to cover up a darker truth. Are you cheating on me? Who were you with?" I continued to block the door.

"Ruby, you need to move."

"Clayton, you never gave me the chance to get to know the real you. I've had to learn you by stumbling up on things."

"Ruby move," he repeated.

"Let me just ask you one more thing," I said. Do you falsely accuse me of cheating on you with random people like the drummer at church, the barber at the barbershop...Oh yeah, I can't forget to mention our nephew, because of the dark truth that you're cheating on me?"

Clayton became enraged and slammed his fist on the door right above my head, then stormed off to the bedroom. I followed behind him, crying for him not to leave so that we could talk. He grabbed my jewelry box and slammed it on the floor, breaking it.

"Clayton, stop!" I screamed.

"I told you to move. You should have just let me leave." Clayton stormed out of our bedroom, then left the house. I fell to the floor while trying to see through the tears to gather my jewelry that had been scattered all over the floor.

Emotionally depleted, I pulled myself up from the floor and dragged myself down the hallway and into the living room. I pushed the door closed that Clayton had left wide opened, and staggered over to the couch and fell on my knees.

"Lord, I need to know what you want me to do with the information you have revealed to me. What am I supposed to do?"

I was totally confused on what I should do next, if I should stay with Clayton or leave him. Yes, Clayton was lying to me, but I had no direct evidence that he was cheating on me. How do you know when it's time to walk away?

I was starting to feel the stress of my tumultuous marriage taking a toll on my mind and body. Three months had passed since the drama unfolded of Clayton's second arrest, and him lying to me about his whereabouts and who he was with, while I visited home.

During the time my son and I visited home, my mother expressed to me that we'd gone entirely too long without seeing one another. She made it a priority to come down to Houston that summer to visit us for the first time.

I definitely did not want my mother to see the mental anguish that I was in, so I put on my best face while she visited us. Although, my body refused to let me hide the pain that I was in from my mother.

I couldn't breathe as my heart raced a thousand times a minute, and pain shot through my chest. I suddenly felt like I was having a heart attack. Clayton quickly drove me to the hospital. My mother and Tyquon were very concerned and came along, too. It hurt when I tried to talk. So I sat in the front of the car silently, and held my hand over my chest while short of breath.

My mother began to pray, "Father God, in the name of Jesus, please touch my baby right now..." She looked at me and said, "It's going to be all right, baby."

We soon arrived at the hospital, and they took me in right away because of the severity of pain I was experiencing in my chest. The pain was so intense that it felt as if my heart was being squeezed to capacity. An oxygen mask was placed over my face and I closed my eyes and thought for a moment: *Perhaps this was God's way of letting me escape the torment of my loveless marriage by taking me home to glory.* However, I looked over at my son with tears in his eyes, and I began to pray within myself for God to ease my pain and allow me to live.

I began to be able to take deeper breaths in, and the pain subsided between each breath I took. The doctors wanted to take an EKG, to make sure that the symptoms I was experiencing wasn't due to a heart attack or some other unknown heart condition. When the doctor came back in with the results of the EKG, he said that everything came back normal. He told me I had the symptoms of an anxiety attack.

"Are you stressed out?" the doctor asked.

I wanted to pull my hair out while screaming, "Yes, yes, and that will be a yes, again!" However, I couldn't answer the doctor's question in total honesty, with my mother sitting right in front of me and Clayton looking across the room at me. My mother had no clue of all of the hell I had been through with Clayton and now wasn't the time to tell her. So, I just said to the doctor, "Well, I have the normal stresses of life that everyone has from working and having a family."

"What are you doing to deal with your stress, to release it?"

"Well, I go to the gym."

The doctor nodded as he jotted on a piece of paper. "I would like to run one more test."

I stopped him. "That won't be necessary. My EKG came back clear, so I know that I'm not suffering from a heart attack. I do not need this hospital bill to go up any higher than it already is." I pulled the oxygen mask from my face and began to sit up.

My mother touched my arm. "Ruby, if he needs to run another test to make sure everything is all right, then let him. Your health is more important than worrying about a hospital bill. You know heart problems run in our family."

My mother had a leaky heart-valve, and Vanessa had to get a pacemaker/defibrillator at the age of twenty-nine.

"I'm okay, now that I know it's not a heart attack. I don't have any insurance, and can't afford for this hospital bill to go up any higher."

"Okay, baby. You probably are just overworking yourself, and you're suffering from exhaustion. You're constantly standing on your feet all day and for countless hours. You probably just need to get some rest, and your body is letting you know that. Maybe you should take a few days off just to get some rest."

"Mommy, I will be all right." I turned to the doctor and said, "Could I please be released from here? That extra test will not be necessary."

The doctor looked at me and said, "All right. I will write a note to excuse you from work for the next couple of days, so that you can stay home and get some rest."

After leaving the hospital, we went directly home. My mother did all of the cleaning and cooking that night, so that

I didn't have to lift a finger. I fell asleep early that night, and returned to work the next day. My mother continued to help out around the house for the remainder of that week, before she returned to Massachusetts. After she left, I desperately tried to figure out, what direction I needed to go in.

I asked myself the question numerous times, *'How does one know when it's time to walk away?'* Perhaps, the physical pain of the anxiety attack was to alert me of the inner pain of my heartache. Nothing gets one's attention more rapidly than physical pain. My pain spoke to me in a loud and clear voice and said, *"Enough is Enough!"* My pain became the evidence that my heart could no longer take the mistreatment.

In addition to the physical pain, the emotional pain had become so great, that I knew a change had to come soon, or my mind would suddenly slip away from me.

I was tired of asking God for the same thing, it had become redundant and seemed as if He had stuck both of His fingers in His ears and was ignoring me. I had to ask myself another question, *"Is God really ignoring me, or am I ignoring God?"* God had already laid out on the table, all that I needed to see about my husband's dishonesty. It was up to *me* with the facts He put before me, to make an intelligent decision that was best for my son and me.

"No matter how much I prayed for God to change Clayton, God was not going to force Clayton against his freewill to love me or even treat me right for that matter," I repeated those same words, until I finally understood. I had to love myself more. I had to be all right with knowing that it was time to walk away, regardless of the funds invested and time wasted, and the love I poured out on him that he blatantly took for granted. I had to be

okay with knowing even if I left him today, and the next day he miraculously became this perfect husband, and rose to stardom in his singing or preaching career, I would be okay. I wouldn't lose my mind because of all that I had invested in him. I was waiting for God to come out and tell me plainly to leave him, but God gave me five good senses, and wanted me to use them for a change.

As a Christian, I had to question if I was so spiritually deep, that I could not make an intelligent earthly decision for myself. Again I ask, "Is there a fine line between faith and insanity?" I was living in insanity by doing the same thing repetitively, and expecting different results. Too often, Christians try to close their natural eyes and ears, and only use their spiritual senses, but revelation comes from a balance of using them both.

My mother-in-law once told me to keep on praying, that God was going to change Clayton, and I believe that she sincerely thought that my prayers as his wife could change him. However, it was time for me to pray for myself, for God to give me the courage to leave a horrible situation that continued to get progressively worse, and tore me apart from the inside out.

After getting out of the shower one particular day, I left to take my son to school, as I normally did on my day off. As I was driving down the street, all of a sudden, I screamed. My vision blurred and I let go of the steering wheel, and started pulling out my hair, while banging my head against the window of the driver's door. The only thing that snapped me back to sanity was the voice of my frantic son saying, "Mom, what are you doing? Are you okay?"

I quickly grabbed the steering wheel and apologized to

him. "I'm sorry. I'm okay. I just had a moment, because I need to get some sleep. I promise you I'm okay and that won't happen again." I reassured my son before he got out of the car to go into his school. However, that whole incident was another wake-up call for me.

I received a call from Vanessa the next day, telling me that she needed to relocate to Houston. She had gone through a horrible divorce, and wanted a clean start to begin her life over with her three daughters. Although my family had no idea of the hardship I had been through in my marriage, I thought it would be good to have some family in Houston with me. I didn't know at the time that God was sending me a support system. I talked to Clayton to see if my sister could stay with us for a few weeks while she interviewed, and found a place to live, and surprisingly he agreed.

My sister got a job at Texas Children's Hospital, and officially relocated to Houston. It was a blessing to finally have some family with me in Texas. The bigger blessing was my mother decided to relocate with my sister to help her with her three daughters. My sister wasn't the only one that needed my mother's help. They didn't know at the time that, I needed my mother's love and support more than they could imagine. I needed that strong woman that I looked up to for as long as I could remember, who had the courage to leave a horrible situation behind many years ago, with five little girls and only a few of our belongings. I needed to feed off of her strength for the days that were ahead of me.

Although my mother and sister lived close to me, I continued to conceal all of the turmoil that I had endured with Clayton from them, until I was sure of when I was leaving him. I was twenty-nine years of age. I could not imagine living the next decade of my thirties, with the same misery I lived with throughout all of my twenties.

I would never advise any young woman going through hell in their marriage, to keep it bottled up inside, especially if it is tearing you down physically or emotionally. You must talk to someone with godly wisdom, who also has a proper balance with earthly reality. I had previously shared the grief that I had to endure in my marriage with a person who was spiritual. They advised me to, "Wait it out, don't give up, keep on praying," and my situation grew progressively worse.

As women we must listen to the voice of our inner discomfort and pain as a warning signal, that a change must come. We take heed to the warning signals on the dashboard of our cars that the oil needs to be changed, or the tire pressure is low and needs more air, but often neglect the warning signs from our bodies. As women we tend to care for and nurture everyone and everything around us, while putting ourselves on the back burner until we become burned out.

If a car begins to shut down and malfunction after its warning signal has been ignored for so long, so will our mind, body and spirit. The stress of an unbalanced and unhealthy relationship will eat away at the core of who you truly are, until you become unrecognizable to yourself, and those around you.

For me, enough was enough, and I was finally ready to take heed of my warning signs.

CHAPTER TWENTY

"Clayton, we need to talk."

It was my day off and I had just dropped my son off at school. It was a good time to talk to Clayton about us going our separate ways.

"Clayton we seriously need to talk." Clayton sat on the couch and totally ignored me.

"Honey, did you hear me? We seriously need to talk," I repeated.

Clayton stared straight ahead and said, "Ruby, I don't feel like talking right now. It can wait until later."

"No, this can't wait until later. We need to talk right now. I can't go on another day like this."

Clayton sighed. "What is it now, Ruby? You always want to start an argument. I was sitting here quiet, just trying to enjoy my day off, and here you go trying to get me all upset."

"That's exactly my point. I've been tip-toeing around you this whole marriage, trying to spare your feelings, at the expense of all of my needs being neglected..."

Clayton quickly interrupted. "I don't want to hear you crying to me about not being intimate with you. You stressing me out has not helped in that area. I never had problems in that area until I met you. You can ask any one of my exes and they'll tell you. I feel like I've been living under a curse ever since I married you."

I shook my head. "So, you're blaming *me* for you not wanting to be intimate with me? I am tired of taking the blame for you being miserable. I try to give you everything to make you happy, but the more I give you, the more miserable you become. And now you're saying you weren't this way until you married me? How low is that, Clayton? All I ever wanted was to make you happy. I left everything behind in Massachusetts for you and nothing makes you happy…"

Clayton interrupted me. "Don't try to act like you left everything behind for me! You said the Lord told you to come down here. I bet you have your family thinking that I forced you to come down here with me. I know you've been talking about me to them. My people back home have called to tell me that your family is going around spreading lies to people by telling them I'm gay. And it's all because you've been blabbing your mouth to them about our intimacy issues every opportunity you get."

"Clayton, that is not the truth. I have not discussed with my family *any* of the issues in our marriage."

He got that deranged look again. "You have even tried to turn my own mother against me, my whole family against me as a matter of fact."

"Clayton, would you stop and listen to yourself? I know that I could never turn your family against you, nor would I ever try. You told me in the beginning of our relationship that I helped bring you and your family back together. Why do you think that I would want to try to put a wedge in between it now? I am so tired of you falsely accusing me about my intentions toward you. I'm going to put your mind to rest once and for all. You don't have to worry about feeling like you're under a curse with me, or that I'm making your life any more miserable than it already is. It's time for us to go our separate ways."

Clayton appeared to be stunned. "So you're just going to leave me here by myself?"

"No, Clayton, I'm not leaving you here. I'm asking you to leave."

Clayton replied, "I'm not going anywhere. My name is on the lease."

"Your name is on the lease but you have not been helping pay any of the bills, and I can't continue to support you any longer."

Clayton seemed unfazed. "I'm not going anywhere as long as my name is on the lease. This is just as much my place as it is yours."

"So, you just expect me to keep on taking care of you, while I'm getting absolutely nothing in return but your black behind to kiss? I am beyond tired. I'm giving you two weeks to find someplace else to live."

"I'm not going anywhere," he repeated.

Clayton meant that. Three months later, he was still refusing to leave. I was beyond miserable.

While the storm of my marriage continued to brew in my home, there was a storm brewing out in the gulf coast by the name of, Hurricane Ike, and there was a call for a mandatory evacuation. At that time, we lived in Seabrook, a town that was surrounded by water and we couldn't risk riding out the storm. We had to evacuate.

I called my mother and sister, so that we could evacuate together. Clayton evacuated with us and took his cousin along. At the time when our family had come together to evacuate for Hurricane Ike, I still hadn't told my mother my plans to separate from Clayton. I was trying to wait to tell her until after he moved out.

Clayton and I took both of our cars to accommodate all of our family. We grabbed some of our belongings such as, nonperishable food, water, clothing, and personal hygiene needs. When it was time to go, traffic was bumper to bumper as everyone in the city was seeking higher ground.

We heard on one of the radio stations that there was a shelter set up in Huntsville, at a high school so we decided to get settled there. No sooner than we had gotten settled into the shelter, the storm hit. Sounds of the hollering wind, along with the terrifying noises of the tree branches that scraped and screeched up against the windows, made it impossible to go to sleep that night.

When morning had finally arrived, the news revealed just how devastating the storm was. Seabrook was among the places that was hit hardest. As we watched the devastation on the news, a feeling of peace rose up in me. That's when I knew that everything was going to be all right.

I spoke those feelings of peace and faith to my family as we watched the news.

"I know it looks bad from what we're looking at on the news, but I just believe that everything is going to be all right at home. God has given me the assurance that it *will* be all right."

Clayton looked at me as if I was crazy. "Ruby, did you just not see that Seabrook is underwater? So you think that

God has angels at the door so the water won't come in and ruin your new furniture?" Clayton laughed at me.

"I know what I'm looking at on the news, but God gave me a sense of peace that everything was going to be all right!"

Clayton laughed again. "I'm glad that you think so."

A few months prior to Hurricane Ike taking place, our apartment complex allowed us to transfer into the unit that was right next door because I wanted more space. I had bought all new furniture after we moved—which was why Clayton made that sarcastic comment.

Clayton had begun to get restless in the shelter and started to pace the floor. I knew it wasn't long before he would begin to go off into one of his crazy rants. He kept on giving my mother and sister dirty looks. Finally, he came up to me.

"I have to go out and get some air. I just can't sit here around phony people. People want to talk bad about me behind my back and then smile in my face like nothing's wrong." Clayton walked away from me, and stormed out of the shelter.

"Did I do something to him?" my mother asked after he stormed out. "Why does he keep looking at me crazy?"

"Mommy, you haven't done anything to him. I've been keeping a lot of things from you that I've been going through in my marriage. I should have talked to you a long time ago, but I just didn't want you worrying about me."

I walked with my mother into the locker room of the high school gym. My sister stayed behind in the gym where the cots were set up, with my son and her children to allow me to talk privately with our mother.

"Mommy, things have not been good. I've been trying to

legally separate from him for a few months now, but he refuses to leave.

"Really?" she asked in shock. "How long has it been bad?"

I lowered my head. "Mommy, I'm ashamed to say, but from the very beginning. Two months after we got married, the intimacy stopped."

"Baby, what do you mean it stopped?"

"Mommy, it literally just stopped. He only sleeps with me once a year, if that."

My mother said, "Oh, baby, I wish you would have talked to me, I would have told you that it wasn't going to work."

"Mommy, I know. I just didn't want to put that burden on you, but it's been really hard. I've been paying all of the bills, except for when he decides to pay the cable bill or the car insurance once in a blue moon…"

I continued to pour out my heart to my mother in the shelter, of all that I had been through with Clayton, including both of his arrests.

"Oh, baby, I am so sorry that you've had to go through all of that by yourself! But you don't have to worry anymore, Mama is here now."

We embraced and cried in the locker room of the gym.

Clayton continued to show the *real* him at the shelter in Huntsville. The secret of our broken marriage was fully exposed to our family in the shelter. Clayton continued to spew out disrespectful rants to me and my mother throughout the duration of the evacuation.

"I don't take well to him disrespecting you, Mommy," I said in anger. My mother had stopped me from confronting Clayton about disrespecting her to her face.

"Baby, you need to calm down. I don't need you getting locked up in Huntsville. He just wants a rise out of you because he knows that he's living on borrowed time in your life."

I listened to my mother's advice. My family and I ignored his craziness until it was time for us to return home.

We got the okay to return home from the news. It was heartbreaking to see the devastation as we drove down the I-45 freeway. There was still a significant amount of debris in the roadways, so we had to proceed with caution. There were a lot of power lines down. We saw a lot of CenterPoint Energy trucks rushing from other states to assist with restoring the power. Although God had given me the assurance that all was well at my place, I was anxious to see with my own eyes if the peace I was feeling was a reality of Him truly speaking to me.

As we drove through Seabrook, everything was in disarray. Debris from parts of people's homes littered the streets. Windows were blown out and missing from various apartments in the Seabrook area. My heart rate began to escalate a few notches as I viewed all of the devastation around us. My heart began to pound even faster as I made a right turn into the parking lot of our apartment complex. The first thing I saw was a boat in the swimming pool.

Clayton and I parked our cars and proceeded to see what we had to face as we entered our apartment. Both of our families followed close behind us, hoping we would have something to go home to.

Our apartment complex suffered a lot of visible damage - windows were blown out of various apartments. As we passed the apartment we had just moved out of, the window was completely blown out, and we could see straight through the apartment, because no one had moved in. The ceiling was caved in and there was water pouring in from the roof.

Clayton turned the keys into the door of our apartment and opened the door. To everyone's surprise, not one drop of water had come into our apartment, and everything was in its place, just the way we had left it.

I began to jump up and down and praise the Lord. My mother and sister began to rejoice with me, and it turned into an all-out praise party. Clayton was furious that we received no damage in the apartment, and the more we praised God, the angrier he had become.

Clayton stormed out of the apartment with an attitude. He knew that his time had officially expired with me, and especially how he'd openly clowned at the shelter in front of my family. It would've made his heart glad if my new furniture had gotten ruined. I continued to praise God for ordering my steps.

The only problem we had to face at home besides Clayton's attitude, was there was no power in the entire apartment complex. My sister, mother, and nieces were anxious to see how they made out at their apartment. So I took all of them home to see if they had suffered any damage. When we arrived at their apartment, everything was just as they had left it, but they, too, had no power.

In my sister's apartment complex, the Red Cross came by twice a day to serve two hot meals for a month straight after the storm, which was perfect because their power was out for about a month.

After I dropped my family off at their place, my son and I headed home. Our neighbors who lived two doors down from us had a generator. He and his wife told us that we can come in whenever we needed to cool down or to get something to eat. My son went to school with both of their sons and was good friends with them, so they let him spend nights over there so that he could stay cool.

Clayton acted normal while we sat at the neighbor's during the day, but when we went back into our apartment at night, he resumed acting weird. On the second night after we returned home from evacuating, Clayton had gone outside by himself for a long time. When he came back in he told me, "Ruby, there's a dead body in one of the cars in the parking lot and that the person looked like she was stabbed."

"What? Did you call the police?"

"No," he casually said.

I didn't know what Clayton was on, but I had begun to feel unsafe. The next morning, I asked, "When are you leaving? It's been long enough. I cannot continue to live like this."

"I told you I am not going anywhere, Ruby. Remember 'til death do us part!"

"So I guess I'm going to have to kill you, Clayton, for you to leave."

"I bet you'll be in a pine box first," Clayton exclaimed.

I took Clayton's words very seriously. The next day after night fell, I went into the kitchen drawer and pulled out a knife and a screwdriver, just in case something went down and I had to defend myself. I had only put those words out the day before in frustration from Clayton not leaving the apartment. I didn't have the capability to kill, nor did I want him to be killed. I just wanted him to leave my life once and for all.

The next morning, a pounding knock woke me up. It was a familiar knock that brought me back to my childhood.

"Is anybody in there?" a female voice yelled.

I went to the door and opened it. "Can I help you?"

"I'm one of the representatives from the health department. This apartment complex has been deemed unsafe, and we're giving all residents three days to find somewhere else to live," she said.

"But I didn't get any damage in my apartment," I told her.

"That may very well be true, but there are a lot of other apartments that did receive water damage, and you can get sick from the mold and bacteria from being in close proximity."

"Okay. Thank you," I said.

As she walked away, I noticed there were other representatives putting notes on every door, condemning the property.

I walked back into the apartment and handed Clayton the note.

"I'm sure you heard that everyone has to leave within three days."

Clayton said with a voice of humility that I hadn't heard from him in a long time, "Honey, where are we going to find a place to move to in three days?"

I fought the urge to laugh and calmly said, "Look, the bus stops here. The free ride is now over. It's time for you to go your way, and I'll go mine."

A sadness filled his voice. "Come on, Ruby. You know that I love you. Now is not a good time for us to separate. Tyquon needs me now. He's about to enter his first year in middle school, and he's going to face all kinds of peer pressure. He's going to need a father figure in his life now."

I couldn't believe Clayton was trying to use my son as bait to keep me with him.

"Tyquon will be all right," I replied.

"Baby, you know I love you." He grabbed both of my arms and rehearsed the same played-out line, "Didn't you tell me that God had put the two of us together? Are you just going to let the devil come in and destroy our marriage?"

"Clayton, I'm not the one that let Satan come in and destroy our marriage. You're the one that left the door wide open for him to come in, when you refused to love me and give me the love that I so desired from you, and very much deserve. You're the one who let him in, when you took my kindness for weakness, and took my love for granted. You've allowed the devil to take permanent residency in our home, and in our marriage, with all of your dishonesty and lies. You've tried to keep me in the dark about certain things, that God has revealed— He's brought it to light. So no, Clayton, I am not letting the devil steal our marriage. You have handed it over to him."

"Come on, Ruby. Maybe the storm was sent so that we could start all over again. Think about it…"

I didn't let him try to finish. "Clayton, you're right. God sent the storm for the both of us to start all over, by ourselves. For you to go your way, and I'll go my way. This free ride is over."

When Clayton saw that I was not budging on my decision, he washed all of his clothes and left that day. I didn't hear from him for a while.

The rescue from my hellish marriage didn't come in the

form of a police escort as it did years ago when my mother left my father. It came from a storm by the name of Ike, and the health department shutting the entire apartment complex down due to the devastation of it.

God sent Hurricane Ike to evict Clayton out of my life, which was long overdue. Some storms are sent to disrupt, shake, and tear things up in one's life, in order to redirect one's path, so that God can start it anew. Those storms are sent in order to shift us into a new season, so that He can rebuild us to take us into our destiny. Storms go against all normalcy of the course of everyday weather. Storms uproot and rearrange structures and landmarks that are viewed as permanent or indestructible, so that all will know that nothing on this earth is permanent.

The only thing that's permanent is God's word, everything else is forever shifting and changing. One must embrace the positive change with optimism, while we learn from the negative changes one encounters, as building blocks for personal growth or incentives for self-improvement. To reject change, is to restrict, then stunt one's growth.

CHAPTER TWENTY-ONE

I had two days left to find a place for my son and me to live. I dropped my son off with my mother and started the search. God led me right back to the apartments where I had filled out an application when I initially planned on leaving Clayton.

I waited patiently as the leasing agent searched her database.

"You're in luck," she said. "Here's a two-bedroom, but it's a townhome instead of an apartment. It has a split-floor plan, but we have a special on this one. This one has a beautiful floor plan. I'll take you over to see it."

When she opened the door, I was amazed at how God upgraded me only in a moment's time. The first room we walked into was the kitchen, which had all stainless steel appliances and granite countertops.

"I love it. I'll take it," I told her once I'd seen the rest of the house.

"Okay great! I'll take you back to the office to fill out the paperwork for this townhome. We need to do a criminal background check and run your credit. If all goes well, it will be all yours. But it will probably take a day or so for us to know."

I didn't have a day or so to wait. I had less than two days to move from our condemned apartment complex in Seabrook. If I ran out of time, I would have to move all of our belongings into storage. Although I wanted to avoid moving twice.

As we rode back to the leasing office, I thought about how I reneged on the two-bedroom apartment in the early Spring. I wondered if that would have any bearings on me getting the townhome.

After we made it back to the leasing office, I sat down at the front desk. My heart began to race as the lady pulled out an application for me to fill out.

"Have you ever been convicted of a crime?"

"No, but I need to tell you that I've already filled out an application for one of the apartments here."

"You have? When did you fill it out?"

"This past Spring."

The tears began to roll down my face all over again. My emotions had gotten the best of me, as I was in a major transition of my life. I was forced to walk away from my husband, the man I loved with every fiber of my being, all because I couldn't make him love me, no matter how hard I tried. In addition, I was being forced out of my place of residency in Seabrook, as a result of the storm. I didn't understand at the time that there was a greater "Force" that was forcing me just where he wanted me to be.

"Was your application rejected for any reason?"

"No. I was approved, everything went through, but…"

More tears began to stream down my face and my words caught in my throat as I tried to tell her my story. She handed me some tissue paper to dry my tears. I took a deep breath and continued. "This past Spring I was trying to separate from my husband. I knew that I should have stuck with my plans, but he convinced me to give it one more try. It's been awful. I hope that it doesn't affect me getting this place. I usually don't renege on my commitments, but he had convinced me that things would be different."

I wiped more tears from my face.

"Please don't cry," she said. "Your application should still be on file. Let me see if I can pull it. Give me your full name and your phone number."

After I had given her my name and phone number she said, "Here it is. I was able to pull it up. Yes, you were approved, and we still have your security deposit from the two-bedroom apartment that we'll use toward your townhome, so you don't have to pay a security deposit. Your background check was also clear then, so I will use this information toward your new application. I am going to go and print up a lease and after you sign it, I will give you the keys to your townhome."

"Are you serious?" I asked.

"Yes, congratulations you're already approved for your townhome."

I broke down and cried some more. "Can I please give you a hug?" I asked her.

She said, "Of course you can."

I embraced her and cried briefly on her shoulders. "Thank you so much for being so understanding of my situation and diligently helping me find a place for me and my son."

"You're more than welcome. Now, I'm going to go and print your new lease out. I'll be back in a little while."

I began to thank God, as the tears continued to shower my face, as I thought on just how good God is.

A few days after my son and I settled into our new place, I received a phone call from Clayton's mother. "Ruby," she said, sounding upset, "I am asking you to please go and see about my child."

"Is he all right? What's going on?"

"Clayton is at Ben Taub Hospital."

"Is he all right? Was he in an accident?"

"No, it's nothing like that. He's all right physically. But he called me saying that he's had a nervous breakdown. He said you leaving him at a time like this, with the storm and all, was just too much for him."

I wanted to tell her if anybody's had or should be having a nervous breakdown, it should've been me from dealing with him all of these years. However, I told her, "You, out of all people, know what I've been going through with Clayton…and for so long. It's been way too much for me to keep going on like this. He's left me no choice."

She said, "I know, but Clayton said that you went down there and changed, that you're not the same person you were before you left. I'm only telling you what he expressed to me."

I couldn't believe my ears. Did she really believe that foolish story? Why would she even entertain the lies Clayton told her that questioned my character now, after all of the years I prayed with her for God to mend my marriage? I learned very quickly that old but valuable lesson, "blood is far thicker than water." I shouldn't have expected her to respond in another manner, as her son pulled on her emotions. Clayton cried out to her and played the victim role. He told his family that they didn't know all of the things I was putting him through because he didn't discuss his marital problems with them. Clayton was very convincing. His mother had to heed to the voice of her son crying from the hospital, about what anguish he was in.

"Have you heard from him?" his mother asked.

"No, the last time I saw or heard from Clayton was the day the health department condemned our place. After I told him I didn't want us to find another place together, he washed his clothes and left, and I hadn't seen him since. He didn't ask me if I needed help cleaning out the apartment, knowing we only had three days to move. He hasn't called to see if we've found a place to live or not. If he really cared, he could've checked on us, but he didn't."

"This is all just too much," she moaned. "I'm all the way up here and can't check on him. Can you please just go and see about my child?"

"I am exhausted. I just finished up moving on a very short notice. I'm getting ready for work now, but I will go and check on him as soon as I get off."

She sounded relieved. "Thank you."

"You're welcome. I'll call you after I leave from seeing him."

I was weighted down with my concerns for Clayton all while I worked. One part of my mind told me that Clayton did this for attention. However, the other part of my mind had true concerns about the state of his emotional well-being. So once I finished working, I quickly jumped on the freeway to drive into Houston to see about Clayton.

When I arrived at the hospital, I went straight to the information desk.

"Can you please tell me what room Clayton Johnson is in?"

"I'll need to see your ID first. And who might you be?"

Sadness filled my voice. "I'm his wife."

She glanced over my license and said, "All right, he's on the third floor in room 304."

When I exited the elevator and came around the corner, I spotted Clayton sitting in a lounging area down the hall from his room. He was sitting on a couch with his feet kicked up, his hands folded behind his head, watching television as if he were at a resort vacationing. An anger instantly rose up in me, as I looked at him sitting there looking rested, as if nothing was wrong with him, while I dragged my worn out and exhausted self through the hospital, trying to make sure that he was okay.

I watched Clayton a while undetected, to see if his countenance would change once he saw I was there. I walked up to him and tried my hardest not to become the unglued person that I felt inside. Clayton's whole posture and demeanor changed instantly once he laid eyes on me. He quickly removed his hands from behind his head and slouched down on the couch.

"Hey Clayton, how are you?" I calmly asked. "What is going on with you?"

Clayton paused. "Ruby, I'm not good at all. I've had a nervous breakdown."

"I am so sorry to hear that, Clayton. I hope that you get better soon. Your mother is really worried about you. She's the one who let me know you were in here. She wanted me to make sure you were all right."

"I was already under a tremendous amount of stress from both of the arrests. Then not being able to make enough money for you, and then the storm. You deciding to leave me at a time like this was just awful timing. All of this is just way too much for me to handle." He sounded so pitiful.

Just then, one of the nurses walked over to see what Clayton wanted for dinner. "I see you have a visitor, and who might this beautiful lady be?"

Clayton said, "This is my wife, Ruby."

"Oh, I'm so glad that you're here," she said. "It's so nice to meet you. He should be going home tomorrow. He'll just need to take it easy. Will you be picking him up tomorrow?"

I wanted to tell her, that's the problem, he's been taking it easy our entire marriage while he watched me struggling to hold everything together. I asked the nurse, "Can I talk to you for a moment?"

"Sure."

We left Clayton sitting on the couch as we walked a little farther down the hallway, in order to talk privately. I kept my voice low so that Clayton wouldn't eavesdrop on our conversation.

"So has Clayton really had a nervous breakdown?"

"No, the doctor has ruled that out. We have him here only to observe him to see if he may be suffering from depression."

"Does depression make you stay out until three and four o'clock in the morning?" I asked.

The nurse had a puzzled look on her face. "Is he staying out all night?"

"Yes." I nodded. "Does depression make you lie to your spouse about your whereabouts, and then come back in the house mean and hostile toward them? Does depression make you dishonest about the money you're making?"

"No, those are not the signs of depression," she replied.

"He wants to claim he's had a nervous breakdown due to me leaving him right after the storm, but I beg to differ. Clayton was not the only one affected by the storm, this affected me and my son as well. When I told him I was leaving him, he just took his stuff and left. He didn't even offer to help me clean out the place, he simply took his belongings and left. And to top everything off, while I was cleaning out his dresser drawers, I came across Clayton's paycheck stubs with the net pay of over a thousand dollars from one pay period. Can you believe that?"

The tears started rolling down my face as I continued to vent to the nurse. "He made me believe he wasn't making any money, all while he rode my back and shoulders to support him. He was real deceitful with it, by only showing me his low check stubs to make me believe he couldn't contribute to his household."

I paused to try to stop the tears from rolling. I swallowed hard, trying to push down my sorrows. "Can you please give me some clarity, nurse. Does depression make you do all of that?"

The woman shook her head in disbelief.

I continued, "I should be the one in this hospital with my feet kicked up, and chilling, while having a nervous breakdown, for the deceit he put me through."

The nurse walked over to the desk and grabbed some tissues. "I am so sorry that you went through all of that.

Maybe you need to talk to somebody, to get yourself some help."

I wiped the tears from my face. "I'll be okay. But to answer your question, no, I will not be picking him up tomorrow."

The nurse looked at me and said, "I totally understand. Please take care of yourself."

I walked back over to Clayton. "I hope you get better sooner, rather than later. Call your mother to let her know that you're okay. She's really concerned about you." And then, I just walked away.

I hurried myself to the elevator, then released another burst of tears once I saw I was the only passenger. As the elevator neared ground level, I quickly wiped my eyes, and took a deep breath before the doors reopened to pull myself together. Once the doors of the elevator opened, I pulled my shoulders back and stuck my chest out, and strutted all the way to my car. I knew that the visit at the hospital would be the last time that I saw Clayton, as his wife, because I was planning on filing for a divorce as soon as possible.

~

Initiating a change, is one of the hardest things to do, and then adjusting to that change comes with its own set of challenges. Although Clayton being gone felt like a thousand-pound gorilla had been lifted off of my back, I hated to admit it, but I missed my husband. I know that it sounds crazy, but sometimes you can become so accustomed to the drama that when it's no longer there, you wonder how you're going to function without the dysfunction. I had become accustomed to Clayton's dysfunction because I loved him so, and was willing to work with all that he came with.

My mind had begun to reflect back on all the intense prayers and fasts I went on in the attempt to get God's attention to save my marriage. I was baffled as to why God didn't save it. What do you do when God decides not to answer your prayers, in the manner that you thought that He should answer them in?

I couldn't answer the question back then and I still struggle with the answer to this question until this day. All I know is that we must keep the faith in Him, because He always knows what's best for us. Our eyesight is limited, but His vision is limitless—He sees far beyond what we can see.

My mother would often spend nights at my townhome, trying to help me get through the rough patches of being a newly separated woman, and also to get some peace and quiet from the noise of my sister's three daughters while living with them. One day my mother sat on the edge of the bed, while watching me restlessly straighten things out in my room, and I said something out loud that I'd only been thinking.

"Mommy, I should just go back to my husband."

My mother tilted her head and looked at me with a stern expression. "And what exactly are you going back to?"

I weighed her words for a minute. "Well, I could just try to make it work again."

She shook her head. "Do you really want to go back to utter misery? It hasn't gotten better all of these years, and it's not going to get any better. And you deserve so much better than that, Baby."

"Mommy, I'll be okay. I'm just about to go and get my husband back."

I guess my mother had enough of listening to my foolish

talking because she said, "Do you want me to knock you upside your head?"

We both looked at each other and burst out laughing hysterically, but my laughter soon gave way to tears.

My mother got up from the bed, embraced me and said, "Oh, Baby, it's going to be okay. God's got you, and Mama's got you, too!"

My mother slept in my bed with me that night and embraced me as she sang songs of worship and I went to sleep.

Four months had gone by since I separated from Clayton. The last time that I heard anything from him was when I went to see about him at the hospital. I think subconsciously I was waiting for Clayton to come crawling back to me, and desperately throw himself at my feet while begging for my forgiveness to take him back. I waited, but I heard not one word from Clayton. As the days, weeks and months slowly began to pass, my clients would often ask, "Did you hear from him yet? Did he call you?"

I would try to appear unfazed. "No, he hasn't called me yet."

When we first separated, they would say, "Oh don't worry, he will be calling you soon, just watch."

But as time began to pass they began to say, "What, you still haven't heard from him yet?" which didn't help me feel any better. I felt the same rejection, if not worse, than when Clayton would turn his back on me and go to sleep throughout our seven-year marriage.

I truly believed that God didn't allow Clayton to come after me because He knew I was not strong enough at the time. I possibly would have let him back in, as crazy as it sounds.

I had to question why I would want someone who had proven to me from the very beginning that he did not love me, want me, or have the slightest interest in me? I had to search deep down inside the inner parts of my mind and heart, and dig way back into my family history. It brought back the memories of my childhood. The majority of my memories of my biological father was that of mistreatment. I had very few happy memories of my father without him yelling to the top of his lungs at us, or beating us excessively. I didn't know at an early age how to vocalize that I wanted peace, or if I really knew the definition of it, but I knew deep down inside that the chaos I was born into didn't feel right. I wanted to feel the opposite of how it made me feel. So, I thought that I could help resolve it by helping my mother out around the house, so that my father wouldn't find an excuse to become angry and jump on her, nor any one of us for that matter. As a result, I became subservient to everyone in my household, in an attempt to try to keep the peace.

I can remember being just short of five-years-old, pulling a foot stool up to the bathroom sink, in order to be able to reach the sink to wash out my two-year-old baby sister's training panties before our father came home from work. She'd come up to me crying and shaking in fear after having an accident in her training underwear. She was in fear of feeling our father's heavy hands of steel crashing down on her backside, and his terrifying voice telling her not to ever wet herself again. Even in my five-year-old mind, I knew that I had to fix it before he came home from work. I would wash her panties in the bathroom sink and hand wring them out the best that I could. Then I'd step down from the foot stool to drag it over to the towel rack, to hang them up to dry. Yes, I learned how to hand wring water from my sister's panties due to us getting in trouble from our father if we left too much water in our washcloths, after taking a bath. He made all of us wring the water out of the washcloths until the palms of our hands were red and sore, until not a drop of water visibly dripped from it. Well, one day after my sister had another accident, I washed and wrung out her panties, then hung them on the bathroom towel rack to dry. However, I forgot to take them down before our father came home from work, and we both had a price to pay. My father went to use the bathroom after coming in from work, and immediately stormed out of the bathroom yelling, "Juanita…did you wet your drawls again?"

My two-year-old baby sister started crying and shook her head no in fear.

My father said, "Yes you did."

My heart dropped when my father pulled the pair of my sister's fuzzy yellow training panties from behind his back, that I had forgotten to take down off the towel rack after they dried. He grabbed my baby sister by one of her arms and yanked her toward him, as his opposite hand came crashing down on her thighs and backside. His voice seemed to have shaken the house and my very soul, as he yelled forcefully, "DIDN'T- I – TELL- YOU -NOT –WET- YOUR- DRAWLS- A- GAIN!"

I cried as I watched my baby sister scream at the top of her lungs as my father went overboard beating her.

My mother stepped in and said, "Leroy, that's quite enough."

My father laid off of my baby sister, then yelled, "WHO

WASHED HER DRAWLS OUT FOR HER?"

I started crying uncontrollably, and he knew immediately, that I was responsible for washing her panties. He snatched me up and started beating me even worse than he beat my baby sister, for trying to cover up her accident. I tried my best to be a good girl, and to do everything that my father told me to do, in order to make him happy, so that no one in the house would have to face his cruel consequences. But no matter how hard I tried, he was never satisfied and always found something to go off on the deep end about.

I ended up in a marriage with someone who was never satisfied with me, too. I wondered if I stayed in my marriage as long as I did, to try to conquer my husband's lack of love for me, as I tried to conquer the lack of love that I felt from my father. I questioned myself over and over again, as to why I waited to leave Clayton? I simply wasn't aware of my worth then. I really didn't understand that I was far more valuable than being subservient or inferior to any other human being. Although I was named Ruby, I didn't know that I was far more of value than what my name really meant, being a woman of virtue. If I only knew then, what I know about myself now, I would have immediately filed for divorce upon separating from Clayton.

However, I finally got the courage to get the ball rolling. I had a client who was a paralegal and she did the paperwork for me. It was a simple divorce because we did not have any children together, nor did we acquire any property or bank accounts together.

Clayton didn't try to contest the divorce, so it was finalized quickly on April the 1st. April Fool's Day solidified that my marriage to Clayton was one miserable joke, and I was a fool for putting up with his foolishness for so long.

I walked out of the courthouse that day, thanking God for bringing me through such a dark period of my life. I was looking forward to walking into the light of a new season. I didn't realize that I was about to walk through another dark cloud of a major storm, and the rain was going to continue to pour down heavily on my family.

CHAPTER TWENTY-TWO

"Yes, Jesus loves me…for the bible tells me so."
    Tears filled my eyes as I listened to the soloist singing my oldest sister's favorite gospel song, from the basement of the same church that I had gotten married in. It was just five months short of my divorce being finalized, and I faced yet another death. Divorce is like grieving over the death of a loved one, but the pain of losing my sister, Lakeisha, was a pain so far beyond my marriage ending, and the feeling was so surreal. To make it even more difficult to cope with, I missed half of my sister's funeral because I was in the basement of the church watching Vanessa's youngest daughter. She could not sit through the funeral due to having oppositional defiant syndrome, and a few other mental health challenges that we were unaware of at the time.
    I agreed to watch my niece until it was time for me to speak, then Vanessa would relieve me. My niece's behavior was so unbearable due to her mental health challenges that we barely made it to the funeral. We almost had gotten kicked off the plane in Houston before the plane had a chance to

take off.

"I'm going to have to ask you to leave," the pilot had said. "That little girl is entirely too loud and she's kicking the seats in front of her, and it's not fair to the rest of the passengers on this flight."

Tears filled my eyes as I pleaded with the pilot and tried to explain the crisis at hand. "Please, we have to make this flight, we're going back home for my sister's funeral. There is something wrong with this little girl, she has mental health issues. Please let us stay on the plane."

The pilot looked at me with frustration. "Well, do you have any medicine to give her, to calm her down?"

I looked at the pilot and said, "I'll try to do my best."

It was not long before we were off beyond the clouds and sailing high in the heavens. My niece finally fell asleep, and we finally had some quiet time. I peered out the window and envisioned Lakeisha flying beside the plane with the whitest wings, along with her beautiful smile on her face, waving and blowing kisses at us. The tears ran down my face as I peered out the window and felt so near to my sister. I reminisced about the time we spent together before I moved to Houston, and how she responded when I told her I was leaving. She cried so hard at the news, as if she would never see me again. I now know why she took the news so hard back then about me moving away. She must have had a premonition that she wouldn't be with us too long after I left.

As I stared out the window, I felt some guilt due to the fact that I was only able to go back home one time before my sister passed away. Although I kept in touch with her over the phone, it wasn't the same as seeing her face to face. I remember one of our phone conversations when I was still married to Clayton.

"Ruby, I had a dream that you were so unhappy and you were crying so hard in the dream."

"Really?" I said.

Lakeisha said, "I don't know why I would have a dream like that. I know you said that God put you and Clayton together. It's probably just a dream."

I wanted to scream out to her, 'I am so miserable.'

However, I concealed my misery from her, and reassured her that I was all right."

Lakeisha had a way of feeling other people's pain, even when they were silent about it. I guess it was because she had encountered so much pain in her life, and at such an early age. It was as if she had a built-in sensory detector for others who suffered in silence with internal, as well as physical pain. Lakeisha was such a strong woman. She kept a smile on her face even through all of the pain that she had to endure on this earth.

As I continued to stare out of the window, the sunshine along with the clouds in the sky became one big blur as the tears filled my eyes to capacity. I was thinking about the last phone conversation I had with Lakeisha, about a week and a half prior to her death. I received a phone call from my youngest sister, Juanita, crying hysterically.

"Ruby, you have to pray for Lakeisha. I don't like the way she's talking."

Juanita had become Lakeisha's caregiver while my mother had moved to Houston. I went into spiritual warfare over my sister, and stayed on the phone praying with her for hours. I called her the next day and she sounded better than she did the night before. It was a total of four consecutive days that I talked and prayed with my sister before that dreadful day she went to the dialysis center, and was rushed from there to the hospital, never for me to hear her voice again. However, when I talked and prayed with Lakeisha the night before she fell into the coma, it was as if she had new life in her. Her faith was renewed and she was talking strong with me, and she shared her future dreams and plans.

"Lakeisha, you're going to be just fine. God is going to raise you up and use you for His glory. What is it that you want to do?"

Lakeisha said, "I want to open up my own soul food restaurant." Lakeisha was an excellent cook. She would always usher the holiday spirit into our family, as she joyfully and strategically planned out all of her holiday meals. She was famous for her candied yams, and took pride in watching her family member's faces light up as our taste buds danced for joy as we ate her cooking.

"Hey, did you ever think about writing a cookbook with all of your recipes?" I asked.

She said, "No, but that's a great idea. What if we collaborated to do a family cook book with all of ours and Mommy's recipes?"

I said, "Yes, that's an even better idea. Better yet, you could write a book about your life, Lakeisha. You've been through so much, that you can help others get through just by your testimony alone. You are truly a living testimony, and I can see you writing books to inspire others through their struggles and difficulties."

I went a little deeper, to tell Lakeisha what I thought God's plans were for her life. I said, "I *know* that God is going to use you to write books of inspiration to others who have suffered like you to help them overcome! You just watch!"

Lakeisha said, "That would be great. I never thought about that."

We talked about all of the wonderful things that God had in store for her. There was the sound of joy and hope in her voice that I hadn't heard in a long time. Juanita had called me shortly after I had finished talking to Lakeisha, and said that it was as if Lakeisha was a new person. Her faith and joy had been restored, and she appeared hopeful for better days ahead of her.

Lakeisha was restricted from the amount of water and liquid she could intake from being a kidney patient. Therefore, she loved eating ice chips to help quench her thirst, so that she wouldn't exceed her daily limitation of liquid consumption. She especially loved to crunch on ice right after she'd come home from dialysis. So Juanita chopped up a whole bunch of ice-cubes into ice-chips, so it would be ready for Lakeisha when she returned home from dialysis that day. Juanita was so hopeful that Lakeisha's health was going to turn around for the better. That day, my sister was rushed from the dialysis center to the ICU. They placed her in a medically induced coma. Toxins had begun to take over all of her major organs and the doctors said it wasn't looking good for her. They gave her only two weeks to live.

After my mother and I received the horrible news in Houston about Lakeisha's gravely ill condition, I knew that Lakeisha needed my mother to be near her, so I sent her.

I received a call from my sister that the function of all of her organs started going up, as if new life was coming back into her body. I praised God and danced for joy all in the salon, as if I were at a Sunday morning worship service.

"I told you that God was going to work a miracle!" I told my sisters over the phone.

We all felt a burst of hope and took this as a definite sign that God was going to raise her up. However, the next day the function of all of her organs went down again, and the doctor told my family that she wouldn't make it through another night.

Juanita went into the room and looked at my sister's lifeless body. She began to scream and cry and choke in disbelief. My family cried together and comforted one another. After Juanita caught her breath for a moment, she threw one of her hands up to heaven, and waved to say good-bye to Lakeisha. For she knew that Lakeisha's spirit was on her way to her new heavenly home, and the old home of her afflicted body could no longer hold her to its pain and suffering. She was finally, "Free at last."

The nurses asked my mother if she, Gail, and Juanita wanted to bathe Lakeisha, and change her gown for the last time. It was entirely too hard for Juanita, so Gail and my mother did. Tears filled my mother's eyes as part of her heart left with Lakeisha.

Immediately after Juanita told me that they pronounced my sister dead, I ran outside in disbelief and fell out on the pavement. I was initially angry with God at the time, because he seemed to ignore yet another one of my prayers.

"Did You really have to take her? It would have made more sense for You to have healed her, rather than take her."

All of a sudden a fear came over me, and I was hushed to a silence. I humbly laid there on the pavement of the patio and cried, "I'm so sorry, Lord. You are God, and I'm not. I must accept what You've allowed."

I laid there and cried for a few more minutes and then pulled myself up from the ground. I went back inside and change out of my nightgown, into regular clothing to drive to Vanessa's apartment to tell her the horrible news about our sister's passing away.

Lakeisha loved to dance, and would dance her pain away. She would turn the radio on and drown out her pain by dancing and twirling, and leaping, then coming down all the way onto the floor in a side split. I could see her now, putting on her silver boom-box with the cassette player sandwiched in the middle of the big, round, black speakers. She would blast Cindy Lauper's song, *"True Colors."*

For some reason, the lyrics were clear as day in my mind. *"You with the sad eyes, don't be discouraged; Oh I realize it's hard to take courage…"*

Lakeisha would leave her cave of sadness and despair, and dance herself into a world where everything was "beautiful like a rainbow." When the music came on and she danced, she let go of all of her pain and heartache and entered into this world where no one else could enter. Neither could any evil enter in there. It was a world where the flowers were so vibrant and never died. The sun would always shine, ever so brightly, and always allow its rays to gently kiss her face as she danced her cares away. The butterflies danced alongside of her, and applauded her as they clapped their wings together for her to give them more. Darkness had no place there, for the light was far too powerful for it to enter in. She had found her place of total peace and freedom when she danced, she had found her place of paradise on earth. Lakeisha had now gotten her wings and she no longer needed to leap in order to escape the pain.

She came to me in a dream the day after she passed away. She had come into the salon and sat down for me to do her hair. Before I moved to Houston, I was the personal hairstylist for all of my sisters, so it was only fitting that I would style her hair for the final time. Gail and I were surrounded by God's peace and Lakeisha's love as we gave her, her final makeover.

As I thought on the days leading up to the funeral, Vanessa came down into the basement of the church with tears in her eyes.

"Ruby, they're calling you up to speak."

I got up from the ground and brushed my dress off after trying to restrain her daughter. I quickly grabbed my notebook with the speech that I had written. As I walked upstairs from the basement, I began to pray for God to give me the courage to speak at my beloved sister's funeral. I quickly opened the French doors of the church as I heard the person officiating the funeral service calling my name for the second time over the microphone. I walked down the long aisle of the church, and someone assisted me up the stairs of the pulpit. As I stood behind the podium and looked down at my sister's casket, and all of the grief stricken faces out in the congregation, I knew that I had to come with words of encouragement and comfort, in order to lift up our heads that hung low.

After I prayed, I quoted Philippians 4:4-8.

"Rejoice in the Lord always: and again I say, Rejoice. Let your moderation be known to all man. The Lord is at hand. Be careful for nothing; but in everything by prayer and supplication with thanksgiving let your request be made known unto God. And the peace of God, that

passes all understanding, shall keep your hearts and minds through Christ Jesus. Finally, whatsoever things are true, whatsoever things are honest, whatsoever things are just, whatsoever things are pure, whatsoever things are lovely, and whatsoever things are of a good report; if there be any virtue, if there be any praise, think on these things."

I took a deep breath, trying to stay strong. "Family and close friends, the Lord wants us to rejoice in Him because God is faithful, and worthy to be praised at *all* times. Some of us may be thinking, *Why would I rejoice right now? What is there to rejoice about? I just lost my daughter, or my sister, or the love of my life, or my best friend, or my home girl, or my counselor.* Yes, I said counselor. Some of us would tell Lakeisha all about our problems, and we'd feel much better after talking to her because by the time she had finished telling us all of her problems and pain, we'd forget all about ours, and start counseling her. We'd realize our situation wasn't so bad after all."

Laughter erupted in the congregation, and people's sadness was turned upside down momentarily.

I continued, "Yes we're all going to miss her, as she has left an empty space in all of our hearts, but God wants us yet to rejoice in Him. Why? Because 'the joy of the Lord is our strength' and it's the only way we'll make it through this. He wants us to rejoice in Him because He is the God that has created us, and He makes no mistakes! He wants us to rejoice for the thirty-years of life that He gave Lakeisha.

God promised man seventy-years, and after that we're living on borrowed time. Lakeisha lived to be thirty-five-years old, exactly half of what was promised, and she demanded love and attention. I believe that she wanted to absorb all of the love and attention that would equal a lifetime, seventy-years and beyond. My sister's and I always wondered why she would grab most of the attention from our mother. I could hear Lakeisha saying, 'My sisters, you'll have your time, but I'm going to get all of Mommy's love while I can.'

Mommy, I want you to know that you gave Lakeisha the love that extended beyond a lifetime.

Your love helped carry her through the many years of sickness and pain. And just when as Lakeisha felt she absorbed a lifetime of your love she said, 'Now I will take my rest.'

So we will rejoice because Lakeisha will no longer have to suffer. We will rejoice, family, because God did answer us. We prayed for the Lord to heal her, and He answered, she is healed. Healed from the pain of this corruptible body. She no longer has to worry about taking her insulin, checking her blood sugar levels, or going to dialysis along with the many pains and discomforts that she had to endure.

Family, now is not the time to let go of our faith! If Jesus delays His coming, we'll all have to die, one day. But death is only a transition, to reposition us into eternity. And if we hold on to our faith, we will be reunited with Lakeisha.

I want to leave this passage of scripture with my family from Romans 8:35-39:

*Who shall separate us from the love of Christ? Shall tribulation, or distress, persecution or famine, nakedness or peril or sword? As it is written for our sake, we are killed all the day long; we are accounted as sheep for the slaughter. Nay, in all things we are more than conquerors through Him who loved us. For I am persuaded that neither death nor life, angels nor principalities, nor powers, nor things present nor things to come. Nor height, nor depth, nor any other creature shall be able to separate us from the love of God which is in Christ Jesus.'"

We said our final farewells to our family, and I embraced my mother a little longer. I knew that she would not be returning to Houston with us, as she now had to raise the two daughters that Lakeisha left behind.

As we were flying back to Houston and I peered out at the darkness that surrounded the plane by the night's sky, I thought about just how much I would miss her. God sent my mother to help fortify and comfort me through the grief of my divorce, and now she was needed to fortify and comfort my nieces through the grief of losing their mother. As the dark clouds rolled past the plane, the tears continued to roll down my face.

CHAPTER TWENTY-THREE

When I returned home from the funeral, there was such an eerie emptiness that clutched deep down in my soul, and I couldn't shake it. I felt so lost at the moment. There seemed to have been too many losses in my life, and far too close to each other for me to try to handle it alone. Within a four-month period, I was divorced, I lost my beloved sister, and lost the company of my mother when she returned to, Massachusetts, to take care of my nieces. I had to find my way through this dark period of time where I felt so alone. Before my mother moved back to, Massachusetts, she was helping me get through my divorce by keeping me company. I thought that I had dealt with the pain of my divorce while she still lived in, Houston. However, I discovered after she had left, I had so much unresolved pain that began to resurface, as I had more time alone to reflect.

My son was at the age where he was pretty much self-sufficient. He'd quickly declined my offers to take him and his friend to the movies, or to game rooms like I did when he was younger. I felt completely lost. For years my sense of purpose was centered around taking care of my son, and being a good wife. Vanessa and her children ended up moving back to Massachusetts, not too long after my mother moved back. Things had suddenly changed drastically. I did not know who I was outside of that nurturing role. I was always at my best when I was catering to others, but aside from it, I did not know what to do with myself. Who was that Ruby who stared back at me in the mirror, I often asked myself? I did not know her, and I felt lost. On top of that, the cold behavior that Clayton displayed when we were married began to play on my mind, and my self-esteem was at an all-time low. It made me think no man would ever desire me.

My thirtieth birthday was quickly approaching. I left Clayton so that I could finally find happiness. I wanted to enjoy, not only the next ten-years of my life, but the rest of the decades ahead of me. I had to get myself together quickly, to embrace the new life that was set before me.

I tried to discover the things that I enjoyed. I always enjoyed working out, so I got a membership to the gym. I found it extremely hard to go out to eat, or to the movies by myself. I felt like people were staring at me with pity saying, "That poor desolate woman…I wonder why she can't find anyone to accompany her."

It was well over a year after my separation from Clayton, and I still struggled with being alone.

Right after my divorce, I thought that God was going to instantly drop a wonderful husband down in my lap, to erase all of the heartache and pain that I had to endure with Clayton. I wasn't necessarily looking for love, but somehow it was looking for me.

This man had the physical appearance of everything I'd ever dreamed of in a man. His name was Corry and he had a body that looked like it was a carved sculpture that the artist poured out his sweat upon, working in overtime to perfect it. His caramel brown skin flawlessly glowed like the dawning of the evening sun, and his smile was simply gorgeous. Not to mention, his mane was curled in the most beautiful locks. His facial hair neatly traced his masculine jawbones, and his mustache laid perfectly around his lips. He happened to be one of the many guys that Clayton accused me of being with. Although, I never had any inappropriate dealings with him while I was married.

Clayton was a self-proclaimed prophet, so maybe he saw a fast forward glimpse of my future when he was accusing me of being with Corry. We started off as friends, but he had always made it crystal clear to me that he wanted to be more than friends. He'd always looked at me as if I was the last appetizer on the tray on a Sunday afternoon, right after coming from a long worship service. So I knew that I was in trouble.

I wanted to honor my commitment to God and abstain from premarital sex, so I made sure that we always met in public places. However, there was a war going on in my mind. The spiritual part of me that loved God with all my heart and soul, wanted to keep His word and abstain from fornication. However, the carnal part of me cried out: *How long will you continue to deprive yourself of happiness? You tried to do things according to the bible with Clayton, and where did that leave you? Loveless and miserable even while you were married.*

I went back and forth numerous times in my mind, from what I know is right, to going after what my body wanted. I think a lot of dedicated Christian women try to avoid the whole dating scene for the simple fact of not wanting to deal with the temptations that comes with it. It's so much easier to avoid fornication when you're not involved with anyone, for the simple fact that you don't have anyone to awaken that sensual part of you that you try so very hard to suppress and avoid. However, I didn't want to be one of the Christians that was so afraid of sinning, that I lived my life in the four walls of the church only, and ceased to *truly* live.

One day I took Corry out to dinner to celebrate his birthday. He was always fun to hang out with, so we always had a great time. The night was still young after we had finished eating, and I had left my car at his apartment so that we could ride together to and from the restaurant. Once we made it back to his place, I planned on getting into my car and going home for the night. He gave me a hug and a kiss and I got into my car and closed the door. He tapped on my window and said, "Hey, why don't you come in for a little while? I promise I won't keep you too long."

Against my better judgement, I said, "Okay, but I can't stay too long, I have to teach Sunday School in the morning."

We started off watching television, but then the television began to watch us as we cleaned up the residue from the dinner we had eaten–from one another's lips. He began to move the kissing down to my breast, and something in me said: *It's time to get up and leave.*

"I'm sorry, but I can't do this. I have to leave," I said.

Corry let out a sigh of frustration. "I don't know why you feel that you don't deserve to feel good, or for someone to love on you. You're a hard working woman and deserve to be loved. Let me love on you this one time, and I promise I won't bother you anymore."

Corry and I were good friends, so I had shared the intimacy issues I went through with Clayton, with him. Big mistake. I realize now, you should never share too much information of your last failed relationship with the next guy because they could use it against you. Your current man could compare all that you've put up with in your last relationship as a comparison guide, to excuse their shortcomings. For instance, if your ex never worked while you were together and you've shared it with your current boyfriend, he could say to excuse his laziness, "At least I work two days a week, your ex didn't work at all."

I told Corry, "I know you would like to make me feel good, and I would love for you to do so, but I cannot be teaching one thing, and living another," I told him.

Corry shook his head in frustration again. "Okay." I could tell he was irritated as he began to put on his shoes to walk me back to my car. Then the war inside of me began.

The carnal side of me screamed, *'Are you going to let this FINE man, who is very much attracted to you, and you to him, just pass you because you want to do the right thing? And just where has doing the right thing gotten you so far?'*

The spiritual side of me said, *'Girl, you better put on your shoes and go so that you can praise God in church tomorrow guilt free.'*

However, I didn't realize at the time that I had some resentment toward God for the way that things turned out in my life. So, I decided to give into what my flesh wanted and my body craved at the time.

"Wait, Corry, I'm going to stay a little longer."

Corry quickly took off his shoes again, and picked me up and brought me into his bedroom. He laid me on his bed, and my heart raced as he hovered over me and took off his shirt to expose his perfectly etched masculine chest. He appeared to be everything a woman could ever imagine. My neglected heart and love-deprived body quickened, as his rough and masculine hands caressed me. He slowly began to unwrap me, like I was the last Hershey's kiss left in the bag that he didn't want to slip through his large fingers, so he handled me with care. He took a dive and was lost in my ocean of love. He dug in deeper to find that lost and buried treasure that was patiently waiting on the bottom of the sea. When he struck it, he knew he couldn't let up, so he continued to dig deeper. He never worried about running out of oxygen in his tank or coming up for any air, for my love that flowed out became the very oxygen that fueled him all the more to love on every inch of my body. My body became weakened by the strength of the love he poured out on me.

I couldn't help but think: *If this was so wrong, then why was I enjoying it so much? Why would God give us sexuality and our human nature only to refrain from it?* I knew all of the answers, that God allowed sex to be enjoyed within the covenant of marriage, but my life didn't turn out that way. So I stopped trying to lay there and analyze in my mind right from wrong any more, and simply enjoyed it. I completely let go and gave into what my body craved. I was lost in ecstasy, as I laid there in disbelief that someone could possibly make me feel as Aretha Franklin sang, "Like a Natural Woman." It felt so good at the time that I was desired by someone, that I didn't have to beg him to show me affection. All while Corry made love to me, he told me how beautiful I was, and how good my body felt to him.

Corry would pause briefly and look into my eyes and say,

"Clayton was a darn fool. He didn't want this? Baby, you have some good…"

Every part of my body felt alive and awakened. Then he held me close and we fell asleep in one another's arms.

The next day, I was on an emotional high, but I felt spiritually convicted by what I had done. Still, there was no denying the love that I felt for Corey. So, I decided to do things my way for a little while to see if I could find happiness. I found happiness all right, but it robbed me of the joy that comes from living a life to please God, by walking in obedience to His Word.

Happiness is only circumstantial. As long as things were good with me and Corry, life was good. But when he failed to come through for the holidays, or do a simple task that I would ask him to do like putting my license plate on my car, it ate away at me and robbed me of my joy. The reason being, I knew that I wasn't supposed to be giving myself to him in the first place. I was again falling into the pattern of trying to make someone into what I wanted him to be for me. I was trying to make Corry into the potential husband that I so desired.

I quickly learned that all men are not meant to be husbands. Some men are just too selfish to commit to sharing their lives with another. The simple things I would ask Corry to do for me, he would always come up short and make excuses on why he couldn't do what I asked of him. Or better yet, he would just simply drop the ball and offer no explanation at all.

I continued to overlook his shortcomings because of the chemistry we had together, and because I fell in love with him. I put my vow of abstinence on pause in search of true love. Although, I was in constant conflict in my mind spiritually. I didn't want to lose him if I decided to go back to living a life of abstinence. What I didn't realize is what I feared of losing the most, would quickly slip through my fingers, especially when I compromised who I truly was to get him in the first place.

That's why it's so important to be equally yoked with someone who is on the same page as you when it comes to being abstinent. Most Christians view the term 'being equally yoked' as just referring to not dating or marrying a non-Christian. However, I learned that you can have two Christians with different value systems, or they had not matured enough in their faith.

One thing about pulling the trailer before the horse and indulging in premarital sex is, you may think you have a stallion in front of your trailer, but in reality all you have is a pony. You're left puzzled, wondering why the trailer is not moving anywhere, and that's because a pony is not built strong enough to pull the weight of your trailer. He is not built to carry you into your destiny.

I eventually realized that after a woman has lowered her standards and indulged in the forbidden fruit of premarital intimacy, she forfeits part of her eyesight. Meaning, we overlook a whole lot of things that we wouldn't have ignored if we weren't emotionally tied to them.

If I had followed this advice, I would have realized that this man complained all of the time, made excuses on why he didn't have money or couldn't manage his money, and was content with just getting by. It took a little more time for me to realize that I deserved more than the crumbs that someone threw out my way. It took even more time for me to realize that as a woman, my body was the gift to the man, and not his body the gift to me. Since my body, my intellect, and the entirety of all that makes me a woman is a gift to the man, I needed to give it to someone who was worthy of receiving it. I needed to give it entirely to the husband that God has especially picked for me, who would protect me, provide for me, and love me perpetually.

Corry continued to make excuses on why he couldn't do the simple things to please me outside of the bedroom. Once I decided to recommit my vow of abstinence to God, and told Corry that he could not move in with me, he found interest in other places with other people. I refused to share a man with another woman. So, I decided to wake up and realize I deserved so much more.

CHAPTER TWENTY-FOUR

As the years began to pass, time became my worst enemy and I felt that God had forgotten me in the wilderness. I wondered if He would ever remember to bring me into the Promised Land. So I wrote this poem, *"Forgotten about."*

Has He really forgotten about me?
Has the One who had formed me from just one thought in
His mind;
Let me slip from His mind?
Causing me to suffer alone in this space in time called life.
With no one to find me,
or someone to be fond of me;
Making me his wife.

Ending one's droughts and those long loveless nights
when one tosses about;
All while rearranging the pillows on the bed
while trying to locate comfort and rest.
And it's nowhere to be found;
Then you become frustrated with the comforter on the bed instead

while kicking it off then pulling it back on;
Because it can't give you the relief of what you're looking for;

Yes, that Amor
that means so much more to those its presence is absent from;
Causing one to crave it like an ice cold glass of water,
in the extreme desert's heat.
And to need it as much as I inhale in, then exhale out;
The free invisible space in the atmosphere, called air.

Relieving me from the loneliness of my hearts despair;
that's brought on by a single heart with no one to care.
Or share any part of your life with;

Whether good or bad, Oh, how I wish I had;
or he would have me.
To be bone of his bone and flesh of his flesh;
the type of love that would forever mesh us together as one.

And me not struggle to deal with this place in time called life alone;
But instead I go day after day, to and dark and cold;
empty and desolate place called home.
Am I the forgotten about rib;
That was taken from of a single and lonely man's ribcage?
When God had once made the decision,
for Adam by giving him an incision;
Then taking out one of his ribs and closing it up;
Along with the hole in his heart;
By giving him Eve.

Then she became his wholesome relief;

Ending his grief and lifetime misery, that is caused by being alone.
Was I that rib, that was laid aside and forgotten about?
With no one to claim me as his dime piece,
Or missing side piece; Or shall I say missing rib piece instead.
I'm missing from the man walking around with the hole in his side;
Needing me whole to complete the empty space by his side.

So shall I ask again, am I forgotten about?

That rib that was laid aside on the ground;
For the dogs to nibble at, carry away, and burry.
Only digging me up at night for his own convenience;
Never bringing me into the light.

How will I ever be found, if I've been broken and buried;
By dogs that are not aware of my purpose.
For if they had known who I am they would have handled me better;

They would not have toyed around and played with me.
Shaking their heads as they nibbled while tossing me about;
Dropping me, then picking me back up;
Covering me up with their dirt;
as they buried me and left me there alone.
Not wanting me, or wanting another to find me;
So I was left buried alone.

But the same dirt they buried me with,
Is the same dirt that God formed me with;
From a single rib from a single man's side.

So God, have you really forgotten about me?

That one lonely rib, waiting for the day that You'd fit me in.
You only laid me on the ground,
So that you could build me from the ground up.
Just like You did in the beginning when You had formed Eve—

So no, God has not forgotten about me!

I had to tell myself repetitive times that God had not forgotten about me. For the simple reason, I felt very forgotten. It was two months after my son and I survived Hurricane Harvey, and the stench of the storm was still fresh in my nostrils.

Neighborhoods were turned into local dumpsites, as personal items from people's homes and businesses were thrown out onto the street. Worst of all, the trash pick-up didn't run for months, so the stench of the garbage along with wet sheetrock, flooring, and other contaminated materials which were thrown out of people's homes and onto the street, made the air almost unbearable to inhale. There were mountains of people's belongings in front of all of the homes and various businesses all around the city. Most of the items looked as if they were barely used, but they were tarnished by the bacteria-infested flood water of Harvey, and therefore deemed as rubbish.

At night it was quite frightening, not knowing what creature or criminal might have been hiding behind the mountain of junk piled in front of the houses in my neighborhood. I was fearful one of the two, were just waiting for the opportunity to jump out and attack me as I came from work at night. I'd quickly run from my car to the house, trying to escape the terror of debris outside, and the stench that offended my nostrils, only to retreat to a home with no walls or floors in the entire lower half of the house.

My refrigerator went out from being partially submerged underwater when the water invaded my home on that dreadful day. Unfortunately, I had to throw out all of my furniture and appliances on the first floor of my house to prevent mold from spreading. I didn't want to buy any new appliances or furniture without the floors to hold them up, or the walls to embrace their welcome. As a result, I was without a refrigerator and furniture for months. I went from eating a healthy and balanced diet before the storm, to eating fried chicken nuggets or Sonic's popcorn chicken. I had to make selections of food that I could eat in one sitting, as I couldn't refrigerate anything left over, and I most certainly didn't plan on throwing it away.

My house didn't feel like a home. I had to fight against the dark clouds of depression that tried to invade my mind and life. In addition, I had to fight the never-ending clouds of sheetrock dust, and other debris particles that filled the air from the walls and the floors being left open. I had developed onset allergies because of it, and it triggered asthmatic-like symptoms that I hadn't experienced for years, because of the poor air quality after the storm. However, I wasn't the only one suffering from allergies and asthmatic-like symptoms. So were many others that were impacted by the storm around the city.

To make matters go from beyond uncomfortable too down-right unacceptable, were the insects that felt they had free rights to my home. They crept and crawled their way through the crevices and cracks of the exposed wood of the opened walls and floors. That's why I was so glad that my son was able to return to his school. A few days after we returned to our home after the storm, I brought him back on campus. It gave me peace to know that he was in a place with walls, floors, a refrigerator, and hot meals from the cafeteria.

Although I was greatly inconvenienced for a while, I thought about the thousands of residents in Houston, who lived in one-story houses, or lived on the first floor of their apartments, who did not have an upstairs to retreat to. Therefore, they could not return to their living-quarters for a while, and for some, because of the severity of the damage and not enough resources to repair them, they never had the option to return at all. Some people were forced into hotel rooms provided by FEMA until a more permanent place of residency came through. Other people who didn't qualify for federal assistance were forced to live with their family members or their friends. I tried to compare my situation with other situations that were far worse than mine, so I could stop feeling sorry for myself. I had to keep telling myself over and over, *"There was no life lost in my household, so I can rebuild. My son and I survived the storm, so what I'm dealing with now, I can overcome."*

I thought of the heroic first responders who lost their lives trying to save others, and brave civilians who stopped making their way to safety to save the lives of others and lost their lives in the process. I was so grateful that my son and I survived, that I continued to downplay my situation to prevent myself from having an emotional meltdown. After the storm, doing hair had become a struggle. Many days I fought back the tears while trying to work.

One day I was so full and could no longer prevent the tears from streaming down my face. My body began to tremble from all I was dealing with, and it was hard for me to breathe. My client told me to have a seat and gave me some water to drink. Then she hugged me tightly, and told me it was going to be all right. I needed to take a break from everything, but I was self-employed, and the bills continued to come in regardless of my circumstances. I refused to set my son back from his graduation track for the following school year, so I had to keep on working to keep him in school. There was such a weight on me as I struggled to figure out life itself. I struggled to figure out why it seemed as though things in my life often turned for the worse. I knew I wasn't perfect, but I always tried to love and help those around me, and live for God the best way that I knew how. As I was restricted to my upstairs, I locked myself in my room every night, as it felt like I was alienated and living in a strange place. It wasn't only the aftermath of dealing with Harvey that had me feeling as though I was on the verge of an emotional breakdown, but the traumatic life altering event that had taken place, only three months prior to Harvey hitting landfall.

I decided to take some online classes beginning in the Fall of 2016, at Liberty University to get my Bachelors in Science and Theology. Around that very same time, something peculiar started happening to me. Every time I would look up to check the time on my cell phone at various times, the time would mysteriously read 8:11 or 9:11. It was as if I was subconsciously programmed to check the time when it fell on the number eleven–hour or the minute. That very same strange occurrence would happen when I looked at the clocks that hung on the walls at the various places that I went. The minute hand always fell on the eleven, and sometimes when I would look up the time fell exactly on the eleventh hour. At first, I took it as only coincidental. However, it began to happen more frequently, and just about every time I thought to look at the time. I began to consistently see the number eleven, not only in the minutes, but also on the hour–the clock read 11:11. I took it as a sign that I was going to lose my life. I know that it seemed pretty extreme for me to jump to that conclusion, but it's how I felt at that particular time in my life. I know that, *"God did not give me the spirit of fear, but of power, love and a sound mind"* (2 Tim. 1:7). However, I let the fear of losing my life grip me every time I looked at the clock and the hand fell on the eleven, whether hour or minute. I began to pray to dismiss the thought of death, but it was always in the back of my mind when I glanced at the clock and saw the number eleven.

Perhaps, the negative thoughts that gripped my mind that something bad was about to happen to me, possibly had nothing to do with the number eleven itself. Perhaps me viewing the number eleven over and over again, was just a symbolization of me viewing all of the trauma I'd been through, over and over again. Perhaps I was viewing the hour glass of my life, and I thought that I was running out of time to fulfill my dreams, and find true love and happiness. I was in search for the answers to the direction my life was going in. I knew that going to school for theology would help me answer life's hardest questions, for the answers always began with God. It was as if God wanted me to be sure of the love He had, not only for me, but for all of humanity before I encountered Hurricane Harvey, and the traumatic events that took place three months prior. My faith in Him was about to be tested with the events that I was about to encounter. For that very reason, God prepared me for a year as I was deep into studying His word.

It was Memorial Day weekend. I had an extremely busy work week, as clients were preparing themselves for the extended three-day holiday weekend ahead of them. Although I was exhausted by the heavy work schedule, I had a sense of satisfaction at how much God allowed me to make to cover the bills. I went home immediately after a late night at the salon on Saturday, and began to work on my theology assignments. I was in module three, of the first-half of the Summer sessions. I fell asleep downstairs doing my homework assignments and woke up early on Sunday morning with a spirit of thanksgiving on my lips. I began to praise God from where He'd brought me from. I began to talk to God and remind Him of what he told me just short of twelve years ago, before I left my hometown of Massachusetts, to move to, Houston.

I prayed, *"Lord, you told me that You would bring me from the wilderness into the promised land. Lord, I've held onto Your promise, and it has sustained me through the wilderness all of these years. Through hell and high waters, I've fought and kept the faith, based on Your word alone to see the promised land. Lord, I feel the promise is in my reach. I feel that it is near, and that I'm at the threshold of entering in the promised land."*

I praised God in advance, as an act of faith from Him shifting me from the wilderness into the promised land, and the presence of God overwhelmed me. I continued to do my homework assignments that were due the following night.

Later on that night, Tyquon wanted to watch a movie

with me. He had just moved back home after completing the Spring semester. After the long holiday workweek, it wasn't long before the movie was watching me. My son gathered his belongings to go upstairs to get ready for bed. I woke up and saw that he was leaving to go upstairs.

"I'm sorry for falling asleep, Ty." I said. "Come on, stay downstairs…I'll stay up and watch the movie with you. I promise I won't fall asleep, this time."

Tyquon said, "Mom, I'm going to bed, and you need to get some rest, too. You're exhausted."

I replied, "Hey Son, I'm okay. I'm just so glad that your home. I missed you…I really wanted to spend time with you."

I continued to beg him to stay downstairs, so I could attempt to watch the movie with him without falling asleep.

"No, Mom. We could watch it tomorrow, and you really need to go to sleep."

After a few times of me trying to convince my son, I finally said, "All right, we'll watch it tomorrow."

I hugged him tightly and said, "It's so good to have you back in the house after a long semester. Good night, son."

"Good night," he said and kissed me on the forehead and headed upstairs to go to bed.

I began to count and organize my earnings from the week. I signed the back of checks of clients who still preferred to use that method of payment, so I could be ready to make a deposit first thing Tuesday morning, when the banks reopened after Memorial Day. After I finished organizing my money, I resumed doing my homework. However, my eyes still were extremely heavy, so I closed my laptop and planned on waking up early to finish before

Monday night's deadline. My purse straps were still around the bend of my forearm, and I kicked my feet up on the couch, and fell asleep on my side. I was partially laying on my purse. I fell into a deep sleep.

It was 4:00am, on Memorial Day, and I was awakened to a silhouette of a man hoovering over me. Only the lighting of the television revealed his image—the dark colored hoodie he wore, with a backpack attached to it.

I began to yell and scream at the top of my lungs, *"JESUS! JESUS! TYQUON, TYQUON GET DOWNSTAIRS. SOMEONE'S IN HERE!"*

The moment the intruder heard me calling for someone to come downstairs, he took off like lightning and ran out of the door. My purse wasn't visible when he was standing over me, so he had already loaded it in his backpack while I was still sound asleep. I was clearly temporarily out of my mind and kept on screaming at the top of my lungs, *"HE TOOK MY PURSE WITH MY WHOLE WEEK'S PAY. I DON'T BELIEVE THIS! OH MY GOD… OH MY GOD. THE BILLS ARE DUE. I DON'T BELIEVE THIS."*

I was in complete shock. All I could think about were the bills, and how I was going to pay them as they were due in a couple of days. By this time, my son was awakened and ran downstairs after hearing the commotion.

"Call the police," I said. "Someone took my purse and ran out the door!" I kept on saying, "I don't believe this. Oh my God, what am I going to do?"

My son stayed calm as long as he could, but after a while could no longer take seeing me in distress and temporarily out of my mind, and he finally broke down. By this time, the police arrived to take a report. Immediately after the cops left, my son embraced me as I could not retain the raw and bitter emotions from my personal space being violated by a home intruder. I noticed that my hand was bruised and swollen as I went into the bathroom to get some tissue to wipe my eyes. While I was still in there, I lifted up my dress to see why my thigh was throbbing with pain. A discovered a big bruise on my upper thigh, about the size of a knee. I assume, in the robber's effort to pry my purse off of my arm, he pressed one of his knees on my left thigh in order to get enough grip and balance to pull it from underneath me. I was in a state of shock, and as numb as the side of the face that the dentist puts the novocaine in, on the day the incident happened. The reason being, not once did I think how the home invasion could've ended in tragedy with my son and me losing our lives. Not a tear ran down my face as the day progressed, but only frustration and anger as I tried to figure out how I was going to pay the monthly bills that were due in only three days.

  The next day, I had awakened to the cold reality of the home invasion and when I stood up to get off of the couch, the strength left in my legs and I hit the floor. The harsh reality of the possible worse-case scenarios, such as my son and me losing our lives hit me like a ship running into an island of jagged rocks in the middle of the ocean, and I sank and felt like I could not rise any more. My whole body began to tremble in fear as I laid on the floor crying hysterically, as I imagined all of the numerous and horrific ways the home invasion could have ended in tragedy for the both of us, and I was mortified.

  I tried to start thanking God for sparing our lives, but then anger took over as I wondered why He would allow something like this to happen us. I took it very personally. By all means, I was in theology school, attempting to do what I thought God was calling me to do. I could not fathom how something like this happened to me being that I wasn't in the wrong place at the wrong time. I was where I should have been, sleeping in my home at four-o'clock in the morning. I began to feel that God Himself was against me, as He clowned me—made a joke out of everything that I was passionate about doing for Him. I always tried to be optimistic, that woman of faith that would often try to paint a light at the end of a tunnel, even if I couldn't see one.

However, it always seemed to lead to more darkness and disappointment, and I was at the end of my rope trying to find the light. I buried my face down in the carpet, and let out a scream that came from deep down in the depths of my belly. It was a scream that came from the very pit of my soul. I had just praised Him on that Sunday morning in faith of Him bringing me into the promised land, just the day before the robbery had taken place. Although I was upset with God, I still knew where all of my strength came from. I continued to ask Him to help me in spite of my frustration and disappointment in Him, for the misfortune that had taken place. There was a major war going on within me, as faith and doubt wrestled in my mind against each other.

Doubt shouted out, "How long will you continue to believe in God, to be knocked into a brick wall every time?"

However, faith shouted out what Job said when his faith was tried, "Although you slay me, yet will I trust you. I will maintain my ways before you."

I picked myself up off of the floor and called my family in, Massachusetts, to tell them of the home invasion. I called my mother and just by me saying the word, "Hello," she immediately detected in my voice that something was wrong.

My mother said, "Baby, what's going on? Are you all right?"

I said, "We're okay, but we had a home invasion."

My mother said, "Oh, my God. Lord Jesus, did y'all get hurt?" I tried to hold my composure so that I wouldn't upset her any further, but my voice continued to break, and I could no longer fight back the tears.

"He took my entire purse with all of my money, and I don't know how I'm going to pay my bills this month. My hand and my thigh had gotten bruised in the process, I know it could have been far worse, but I just don't understand why God would allow this to happen to me. I have tried my best to keep the faith through it all, through everything I had gone through with Clayton…" I paused for a moment to let out a sigh of frustration. "I just don't get it," I continued.

My mother interrupted me with outrage and disbelief, "He actually touched you? He could have killed you." She started thanking and praising God for sparing our lives. "Hold tight, baby, Mama will be there soon. I do not want you going through this by yourself, this is just too much."

My family was outraged by the incident and pooled all of their money together to send my mother to me for a month. Her plane ticket was set for only eight days after the incident occurred, and I anxiously awaited her arrival since she always had a way of making the most stressful more bearable.

After I had gotten off of the phone with my mother, I continued to wrestle with the dark clouds of doubt and depression that tried to choke out the light of my faith.

Doubt shouted out, *"Let go…You can't take it anymore!"*

I got down on my knees in the same room I was robbed in, and attempted to pray. However, my knees could not hold up the weight of my burden, so I stretched out on the floor on my belly and the only words that came out was, "Lord… I'm tired."

As I laid on the carpet, all of the horrible things I went through in life flashed before my eyes. Satan began to speak to me loudly, in the form of the voice of doubt, to make me give up my faith in God.

The voice of doubt said, *"God sent you down to Houston on a suicide mission. Just think about it, every attempt you make to move forward ends up in ruin. God's trying to kill you in the wilderness because there is no promised land, so stop fooling yourself. God has turned a deaf ear to all of your prayers. That's why everything you pray for goes in the opposite direction that you pray for it to go in. Look at how hard and long you prayed for your marriage to be fixed, and that ended in ruin. What about how hard you had prayed for your sister to be healed and live, and God ignored that prayer, too. Clearly, Ruby, there is no promised land. Every road you get on in hopes of finding the promised land leads to an abrupt and painful dead end."*

In the moment of my weakness, the voice of doubt was strong. "God has failed you. Give up now to avoid any further heartbreak and disappointment."

I laid there weak and almost lifeless as the lies that the enemy told me began to zap what little bit of strength I had left within me. As the tears began to saturate the carpet, the voice of faith began to reason within me. The voice of faith began to give me clarity, and I was able to think on these thoughts:

"In spite of all the misfortune and disappointment in my life, God never allowed it to destroy my son or me. I began to think to myself, if

God really wanted me dead, as the voice of doubt tried to convince me, then I would not be here right now."

The voice of faith that was rooted deep down within me from the time I was a little girl and watched my mother walk by faith, gave me the strength to muster up the words that Job said when he was tested, *"The Lord gave, and the Lord hath taken away; blessed be the name of the Lord."*

As I began to bless God in spite of my present calamity, the voice of doubt slowly began to fade out. The voice of faith became the dominant voice within, drowning out the voice of doubt momentarily. The voice of faith began to reason within me, to remind me of how over the years God had always showed up on the scene to interrupt the plans of the enemy from coming to full fruition.

The voice of faith spoke with authority and said, *"Although the enemy formed many weapons against you, not one of them prospered and destroyed you."* At that very moment, the voice of faith gave me some clarity to move some of the dark clouds of doubt out of my mind. It gave me the strength to get up off of the floor and go and handle my business, even though I struggled from moment to moment, from being shaken up by the entire incident.

The first place I went to was the DPS office to report my license stolen, and to replace it. I forced a smile as I took the replacement license picture, but the dazed look in my eyes told the story of the trauma I had just gone through the day before.

Some might view walking by faith, as if you're always walking around painlessly with a bright and wide genuine smile on your face. As though all of your problems and Satan himself is underneath your feet, as you're standing on top of the world. However, that is a false personification of the reality of faith. There are times when walking by faith that you've cried all night, and have to force a smile on your face to cover the reality of the pain consuming your heart as you go throughout the day. So that you won't wipe out the hope and joy you see in other believers' eyes by the reality of your sadness. There are times when walking by faith, when it seems as though you're walking all alone and barely moving, while the whole world is effortlessly passing you by. It may bring you to a rough and rugged, uncharted and uphill road unbeknown to you or anyone in your family, as you're struggling and fighting to maintain the grip underneath your feet, to continue moving forward as you're climbing the road of faith to make it to your destination. There are times when walking by faith, that you may lose your footing along the way, and fall down and get bruised up or cut up by the jagged rocks of life's circumstances, and the fear and pain of that fall will often paralyze you to prevent you from moving forward. Yes, it's ok to pause for a moment in order to regroup and to tend to your wounds, but the key is not to give up. Donnie McClurkin sang, "*We Fall Down, but we get up.*"

We have to "Get Up" in order to progress on our faith journey. The greatest people fall down numerous times. However, they muster up the strength to get up and pursue something far greater than the cold ground beneath them. As long as you fall on top of the ground and not underneath it, you'll have the opportunity to get up from wherever you've fallen, and propel forward toward fulfilling your dreams.

I was barely moving the day after the home invasion, but I had to continue to take care of my business. After stopping at the DPS to replace my license, I went to the bank and had new bank cards issued and ordered new checkbooks. I was a nervous wreck as I fumbled through my purse to find the temporary paper license I had taken only minutes ago, at the DPS. To make things more terrifying for me, the criminal waited a couple of days after the home invasion and tried to use my card at the local Walgreens. It failed to go through because I had already cancelled it. This confirmed the urgency that I had to move from the place I was robbed in, with the fear that the criminal who invaded my home would come back. Either he lived in the area, or frequented the area on a regular basis. The anxiety that I already had heightened all the more.

I immediately went home and started the process of packing up our apartment. After I cleaned out drawers and threw things away to prepare to move, I attempted to look at my theology assignments for the week. I didn't want to fall behind because it's almost impossible to get caught up if you do.

CHAPTER TWENTY-FIVE

I called Liberty University the next day to see if I could get an extension on my assignments. I explained the entire situation, and told them that I was in the process of finding another place to move to. They prayed with me over the phone for God's guidance and strength in the situation. As soon as I hung up the phone, I emailed both of my professors to let them know of the trauma I'd gone through, to see if they could give me extra time to complete my assignments. Both of my professors for my summer courses gave me a two-week extension on my assignments. Then I had the time to focus on moving. At the time I had no clue of where I was going to move to. All I knew was, I did not want to move to another apartment setting.

When I went to work, I was still in a daze from dealing with the post-traumatic stress of the home invasion. My first client, who was a realtor, saw the residue of the trauma still left on my face.

She said, "Hey Ruby. Are you alright? You're not looking like yourself today."

"Mrs. Karen, I had a home invasion on Memorial Day

morning. He took my purse with everything in it, and bruised my thigh and my hand. I could barely close my hand, it's in so much pain."

Mrs. Karen said, "Oh my, Lord. Ruby, why are you here? You need to be somewhere resting and taking care of yourself. Is your son all right?"

"My son is fine, thank God. He was upstairs sleeping at the time the incident took place. I don't even want to think of how it could have ended up had he been downstairs with me. I'll be okay. I'm going to have to work with this hand the best I can. You know how it is being self-employed—if you don't work you don't eat."

My client gave me a hug and said, "Ruby, you have to get out of those apartments. Have you found another place already?"

"No," I said.

"After I leave here, I'm going to go to the office and pull up some listings and I'll call you," she said.

Mrs. Karen picked me up on Sunday with her beautiful granddaughter Kayla, but that day we couldn't find anything that was right for my son and me. She picked me up early the next day, and the first house we viewed was nice looking, but it had too much wooded area in the back of it, and my nerves were too bad after the home invasion to live there. The second house we went to had a cozy and inviting atmosphere. Immediately upon us walking in, Mrs. Karen's granddaughter started dancing and twirling around in the house, showing so much joy and excitement over it. I took her excitement and joy as a good sign that the house was the one I was supposed to get, because the other houses that we looked at, Kayla was afraid to enter into the next room without us.

"This is completely out of her character, she's usually shy and reserved. This must be the one," Mrs. Karen said.

The place felt nice and cozy, like it was supposed to be home for my son and me. After we left the house, Mrs. Karen brought me back to her office to fill out the application to see if I'd get approved.

"All we have to do is wait to hear back from them to see if you were approved. You should be hearing from them at the end of the day or tomorrow," She said. She took me back to my place, which was right down the street from her office.

"Thank you so much for everything, Mrs. Karen. And thank you, Kayla, for that beautiful dance."

Kayla smiled at me and said, "You're welcome, Mrs. Ruby."

"Try to get some rest, and make sure you get yourself something to eat," Mrs. Karen said.

I didn't have an appetite and it was starting to show, as the weight began to drop off me from stress. I was sleep deprived and running off fumes and sheer adrenaline, and it clearly showed. I was just about to get into my car to go drop off the money to pay my booth rental fees at the shop, when Steve called. Steve owned the business that I worked in.

"I need you to bring the booth rent up here now. I need to pay the bills."

That just made me snap.

"Didn't I tell you that I was going to bring the booth rent to you today? Don't worry, I'm coming now!"

I couldn't believe that he was being so impatient knowing the situation I had just been through. I'd never been late before, and he couldn't show me an ounce of compassion.

I sped to the shop and jumped out of the car, almost

ripping the door off of the building as I went in.

"Didn't I tell you that I was going to give you the money today?" I yelled at Steve, who was sitting in his barbering chair. I shoved the money into his hand.

"Dang, Ruby," he replied, "Are you on your cycle?"

"No, did you forget? I just got robbed, and I've been out looking to find somewhere else to live. Have you any patience?"

I stomped back out the door, got into my car, and broke down crying. I was on edge and at my wits' end. It was exactly a week since the robbery, and I still couldn't think rationally or logically. Satan knows when to get to you when you're not only spiritually exhausted, but when you're physically and emotionally depleted of strength. I wondered what was the point in living life anymore, when all my efforts to do the right thing always seemed to end up in turmoil. Satan, in the form of the voice of doubt, returned to rehearse those same words he spoke to me the day after the home invasion. The voice of doubt spoke louder than ever before and said, *"God sent you down here on a suicide mission. Everything you try to do is going to end up in disaster. The mission is impossible. You might as well end your life now. Clearly God is against you. You're on a suicide mission."*

I sped off from the salon and revved my engine as I was speeding down the street going eighty to ninety miles an hour. Juanita called and I started not to answer the phone, but something (God) made me pick it up.

Juanita had a sense that something was horribly wrong with me and she said, "Ruby, are you all right?"

I continued to speed with the intentions of driving into a tree in order to end my life. I screamed out, "I'm tired! All the good I do ends up in ruin. Nothing ever turns out right in my life. I'm tired! It's so obvious that God is against me."

Juanita began to cry and said, "Ruby, please calm down. It's going to get better." She began to pray. "Jesus, please help my sister…"

As Juanita continued to cry and pray, something (God) told me to pull into a parking lot of a building I was about to pass up. It wasn't even two minutes from the time I pulled in, that I had a call on the other line. I clicked over and answered, not bothering to hide the exhaustion in my voice.

"Hello," I answered.

"Hi, Mrs. Sanders," a female voice said. "I just wanted you to know that you've been approved for the house. You can pick up the keys and move in on Friday."

I let out a sigh of relief. "Okay, thank you. Thank you." I switched the call back over to my sister and told her that I was approved to move into the house.

"See, Ruby, God is with you. Please don't ever scare me like that again. I felt like I would never hear from you or see you again," Juanita said.

Juanita could not actually hear my engine revving up. Neither did I tell her at the time she called, that I was getting ready to drive into a tree to end my life. Only God alerted her that I was in distress. I was temporarily out of my sound mind from trauma and exhaustion. I almost made a permanent decision based on a temporary circumstance. In a moment of hopelessness, Satan almost convinced me to end my life.

A suicidal mind is so intoxicated with hopelessness that you cannot clearly see another solution to escape your moment of hopelessness other than death. So you make a permanent decision, based on a moment of hopelessness. A moment is a is defined as brief period of time. Meaning, the feeling of hopelessness will eventually pass away. The way out of my moment of hopelessness was only two minutes away, when I received that phone call telling me that I was approved to move in. Had I given into that moment of hopelessness by driving into a tree, as my exhausted mind told me to do so, I would have never been able to see that my solution was right around the corner. I was literally two minutes away. I would have left my son heartbroken and feeling lost, along with the rest of my family and loved ones, when my solution was only two minutes away. The suicidal mind that I had was brought on by the trauma I had gone through, as I suffered from exhaustion due to sleep deprivation. Life is a precious gift. Always choose life.

I immediately called Mrs. Karen to tell her that I was approved, and thanked her for all of her help. I called Steve at the salon to apologize for the attitude I displayed to him. I explained to him that I hadn't had any sleep since the robbery, and I was exhausted trying to find another place to live. Steve quickly accepted my apology, so I believed that all was well at the salon.

My mother arrived in Houston the next day, and my son picked her up from the airport and brought her to the salon to see me while I was working. My mother embraced me, but I saw the worry in her eyes as she looked into mine. She fought back the tears.

"Baby, are you okay?"

"I am now that you're here."

We embraced again and she said, "You have to get some rest, you look exhausted."

I said, "As soon as I get out of that apartment, I'll be able to."

After I left work, my mother made me lay down while she continued the work of packing my apartment. As I laid on the couch, I prayed trying to figure out how I was going to get the money to pay for June's rent, which was almost nine days overdue. I was still responsible for paying it, even though I was robbed at the apartment complex. As I laid there in prayer, something (God) told me to send out a mass text to my friends and clients to ask for help. As a giver, asking for help went against everything within me, and I cringed at the very thought of it. I had never asked clients or friends for monetary help, and I feared that I would lose them as a result. I tossed and turned on the couch as the thought for me to send out a mass text for help, kept strongly weighing on my mind. I had to push my pride aside, and I finally said, "Okay, yes, Lord."

I sat up on the couch and began to text:

On Memorial Day, at 4:00am in the morning, I woke up to a home intruder standing over me. He took my purse with all of my earnings I made for the holiday week, and I have not been able to pay my bills for the month. All of those who know me, know it's totally out of my character to ask for any monetary help, but under the circumstances I am soliciting your help. I will greatly appreciate whatever God puts on your heart whether big or small. No amount is too small to give. Thank you in advance for your help.

After I typed up the text, I held the phone and stared at it. Finally, I said, "I trust you Lord," and hit Send. My heart dropped and then raced, then my palms became very sweaty from the uncertainties of the responses that I would receive. It wasn't long before my phone started dinging with nothing

but positive responses:
Don't worry, I have you.
I'll stop by the shop tomorrow.
Come by my job, I'll have something for you.

Those who couldn't give a monetary gift, called or texted with encouragement that me and my son were in their prayers. Some even took the time out of their day to actually pray with me over the phone. By the end of that workweek, I was so overwhelmed with the love that was poured out on me by clients and friends, that all I could do was weep tears of joy and gratitude. Different people stopped by the salon while I worked, and just about every one of them handed me one hundred dollars. Others came with envelopes that contained a couple of hundreds or more inside. One friend told me to pick up some money from her job, and as I was on my way, my car stalled out and stopped. She and her husband had my car fixed free of charge, and still gave me a monetary gift on top of that. Another person took my son to get tires, and gave him some money to go toward his summer tuition.

God works through people, and the love that He showed me through them, solidifies that He truly loves me. It cancelled out all of the lies of the enemy, that implied that God was against me. People were willing to give so much until I gained everything back that I lost when the home intruder stole my purse, plus double of that. People were still trying to give the following week, but I refused to take anything else. There were some who did not get a chance to give to me the week that I sent out the text message, so they insisted on giving, and refused to take no for an answer.

I moved on a Sunday to avoid taking off from work. Furthermore, most of the people who were helping me move worked on Saturday, too. That's why Sunday worked out best for everyone.

I heard a knock on the door and the first one to arrive to help me move was one of the barbers, who used to work at Steve's shop. Then a few of my son's friends came to help. After a while, a coworker from Steve's barbershop came with all of his tools and two of his nephews and started disassembling our beds and dressers to load them on the truck. A friend came with her daughter to show their support. After a while, I had a whole moving crew of caring and concerned friends who just wanted to make sure that I was out of that apartment complex, and in a safe and secure place.

I ordered pizza and Popeyes chicken to feed everyone who helped me move. By the end of the night I was completely moved out of the apartment, with the exception of a few small things that I had picked up when I returned the keys to the leasing office the next day. I quickly handed the keys over to them and never looked back.

The bible says, *"Ask and it shall be given to you. Seek and you will find. Knock and the door will be opened unto you."* I swallowed my pride and *"asked"* for help, as God put on my heart to do. As a result of obeying Him, I was able to pay not only the rent and the late fees at the apartment that I moved out of, I also was able to pay the first month's rent and security deposit to the house that I moved into, and still have extra. God blew my mind and poured out upon me an "exceedingly and abundantly above all I could ask or think," type of blessing. (Eph. 3:20). God used my client and friend, Mrs. Karen, to help me *"seek"* a new place of residency for my son and me, and we *"found it."*

I was about to enter into a place of *"knocking"* on a door

that I wasn't anticipating knocking on at the time. But when God says it's time, all things will line up to fulfill His word. God shuts down doors, to allow you to walk through the door that is destined for you to walk through.

The next day was the start of my workweek. Although I was still exhausted from the move, it was a good feeling just knowing that I was out of the apartment I was robbed in. I had anticipated getting adequate rest from the insomnia I had been dealing with since the robbery.

I walked into the salon and while I was waiting for my first client to arrive, Steve walked in.

"Ruby, we have a mandatory meeting this afternoon and it's imperative that you be here," he said.

From the look on his face, I knew that it wasn't any news I wanted to hear. So I asked him, "Steve, can you please tell me what's going on? I am exhausted from moving over the weekend. My nerves are really bad right now from everything I've been through over the past couple of weeks, and I do not need any more surprises. Can you please tell me if I need to look for another salon to work in, and if so, how long do I have to look? You know I have a son in college to support, and I need to know if this meeting will affect my livelihood."

Steve sighed like he really didn't want to go into any details right then. Even still, he said, "The option to stay is yours if you want, but I have sold the shop to someone else."

I went from one crisis to the next. I went home and told my mother of the other hurdle I was up against, that I needed to find another salon to work in.

"Baby, this is just too much, you have to get some rest."

"I know, Mommy," I replied. "I'll be able to get some rest after I finish out the semester, and find somewhere else to work."

My mother immediately went into prayer for God to give me strength. She feared that I was at the point of breaking from the pressure that I was under.

The next day when I went to work and had a break in between clients, God put it on my heart not to look for another salon to work in, but instead, to look for a location to open up my own salon. I had been in the hair industry for twenty years and every time I left a salon, it was because of the negligence of the owner not taking care of their business properly. I was a person of stability and did not want to rely on how another person's ability to run their establishment sufficiently, or insufficiently, to affect me. It was far past the time for me to take control of my life, with the twenty-years of experience that I had in the hair industry by opening up my own business.

I immediately went to a business center that wasn't far from the salon I was at, and knocked on the door of the business office. One of the office managers opened the door and answered, "How can I help you?"

"I am in dire need of renting a space to open up a salon," I told him.

"How much space do you need, and when are you looking to move in?"

I answered, "I need space for about two stylists to operate in. Not too big, but enough room to be able to move around in to accommodate our clientele comfortably."

I had a friend in mind that I wanted to be my business partner. Her name was Carla, and we worked together quite well when I first moved to work at Steve's establishment. She left Steve's establishment to open up her own salon, but eventually outgrew the space she was in. She then moved to rent out a booth in another salon not too far from where I worked. We'd always kept in touch and maintained our friendship throughout the years. In pass times, we attempted to look for a location to open up a salon together in, but we couldn't find anything within our budget or in the same area that we had built our clientele in. Therefore, we had to put our plans on hold.

However, timing is everything. The manager took me over to one of the buildings that had plenty of space for both Carla and me. In addition, it had an upstairs and downstairs if we wanted to rent out a booth to other hairstylists.

The manager who showed me the space asked, "So what do you think? Is this space something you would be interested in getting?"

I asked, "Can you please give me a day or two to think about it?" I wanted to show it to Carla to see what she thought about it."

The manager agreed that it was okay. I immediately contacted Carla with the exciting news.

"Hey Carla! We're about to open up our own salon!"

"Are you serious?" Carla said.

"You know we've looked a couple of times for a building in the past, and every place we went was sky high," I told her.

She answered, "Yes."

"Well, I just found something with plenty of space, at a great price, and we could even rent out booths to other hairstylists if we choose to do so."

"Oh my, God! What made you decide to look right now?"

Carla had just gotten back from her destination wedding

and honeymoon in the Dominican Republic. I gave her a brief update of the recent crisis I had been through with the home invasion and then Steve selling the shop. I told her that I didn't want to look for another salon to work in, that I was ready to open my own salon, and I wanted her to be my business partner. So Carla agreed to go and view the space with me. After she saw it, she made a valid point that the stairs would be too much for our elderly clients to climb. The manager showed us another space that we both didn't agree upon. Carla said that she would extend her search for a building beyond the location of the business center that we were looking in, to broaden our options.

My mind went back to the business meeting with the man who was supposed to be taking over for Steve. Steve wanted us to meet the man who was scheduled to take over his business in two weeks. Steve sat in on the meeting and allowed the soon to be business owner to disrespect me, and left me livid.

"So Ruby, I hear that Steve can't fill this other styling chair because you can't get along with anybody," he'd said.

"That's not true. I've been working in the beauty industry for twenty years now, and this is the first time I've worked alone," I replied.

"I've heard it from several people that you like to run things, and you run away anyone who inquire about renting a booth here." He smirked like he had me all figured out.

The only person who could've told him this false information was Steve. Steve was upset with me because I told him that he could have given us all a heads-up about selling his business. We all had been working there a number of years and we viewed one another as family, rather than coworkers. He didn't like the fact that I called him out and told him he should have considered any one of us to sell his business to.

I glanced over at Steve to let him know that I was aware that he fed the new business owner this false information and said, "Your 'source' has the story all wrong." I turned back to the business owner and continued, "I've been loyal to Steve, and this establishment for years. I'm not the reason this styling chair is not filled. Steve won't make the proper adjustments to fix it up back here. The only reason why the salon area was recently painted is because I told Steve that we needed to fix it up, if he wanted to rent out the other styling chair." I spoke the truth and didn't care that Steve was sitting right there.

"I need to know right now, who's staying or whose leaving, Ruby?" The immature so-called business man turned to me with the look of arrogance in his eyes.

"I need some time to think about it. I just went through a lot and I need some time to make-" He cut me off.

He barked, "Dang, Ruby!" It's not all about you. I have a family to feed. Stop being difficult. I need to know now if you're staying or leaving?"

"I told you I need time to think about-"

He interrupted me again. "You should be grateful that Steve sold the business to me to keep the doors open. Where else would you have to go since you're so difficult to work with?"

I schooled him, "You need to learn how to listen, if you want to run a successful business. Furthermore, I am a licensed hairstylist with twenty-years of experience. I could go anywhere to work."

He continued to poke at me. "Oh yeah, and where would that be?"

As hard as it was, I held my composure in order to keep it professional until the meeting concluded. I was already looking to move, but this encounter with the new business owner sealed the deal. Especially with Steve sitting there, allowing someone to come in and talk to me any kind of way, after I was loyal to him for years. I still needed a place to work until I found a location. I never burn my bridges, so if worse came to worst, I could work in the salon I worked in before I moved to Steve's establishment.

I went home that night and told my mother all that had transpired at the meeting. She immediately went into prayer for me, as she could see the stress and pressure I was under. She prayed that God would lead me to the location of the business that He wanted me to be at. She concluded the prayer with these words, "Lord, we're asking you to shut every door that needs to be shut, and open the door that she needs to walk through, in Jesus' name, Amen."

The next day I went back to work and God put it on my heart to go back to the same business center I had gone to before. I *"knocked"* on the office door once again, and the same office manager was there, and I poured my heart out to him.

"Sir, I am in desperate need of finding space here to open a salon. I just moved my residence a little over a week ago because of a home invasion, only to find out that the owner of the salon I'm working in is selling it. I need a safe environment for me, and the clients that I service." I became emotional as the tears flowed down my face. "Can you please help me find a space?"

"I'm so sorry to hear that you're going through all of that," the manager said. "There is a spot that just became available that is fully renovated. All you would have to get is plumbing to install your sinks. I'll take you down there right now. It's a one-level like you wanted, but it's not as big as the other suites you looked at before. But I think it's plenty enough space for you to operate in, and it even has a small waiting area. When he opened the door and we walked in, I knew that it was *"the door"* that my mother had prayed only the night before for God to open, that I was supposed to walk through.

"The only reason why this space is available now is because somehow it wasn't listed." he said.

I wanted to shout and praise God all over the building because I knew that the "somehow" reason the building wasn't listed was the Lord was making a way for me to open a business "somehow."

"You'll have to make the decision right now, or otherwise this space will be listed his afternoon. I know you're going through a lot, so I will try my best to make it affordable for you. I'll only add a fifty-dollar increase each year, on a three-year contract, if you were to accept it."

It was six to eight hundred dollars less than the other spots that we looked at. I had to realize that this was my moment to take a leap of faith. It was as if the lights came on and I had what Oprah Winfrey defines as an "aha moment."

It was at that moment that I realized that all that I had been through in my life, had prepared me for that very moment. I did not have time to think about all of the details that went into opening a business. I had to make a decision based on my faith in God and simply trust that He would work out the rest of the details later. Therefore, I stepped out on faith and told him, "Yes, I want to rent this space."

"Great!" he replied. "The owner of the building will be coming down tomorrow, and I just have to wait to see if he will approve it for the price I offered you."

I left the place thanking God in advance, as an act of faith, that it was already mine. I finished up my workday and went home, and told my mother of the deal that the manager at the business center offered me. We rejoiced together, and praised God in advance for allowing it to come through, even though it wasn't official until the owner approved it.

The next day, I went to the business center to meet the owner himself. He shook my hand and said, "I just have to shake the hand of the person that this man bugged me nonstop to find a space for. He gave me grief about giving you this space. I agree to give you this spot at the price he offered you, but you have to take it as it is. It is already fully renovated, look at how beautiful it is. I just love these French doors." He paused for a moment and asked, "This is going to be a salon, right?"

I nodded. "Yes sir."

He continued, "You'll need plumbing for your sinks, right?"

"Yes sir, I do."

"I am going to throw in two lines of plumbing free of charge."

My mouth hit the floor along with the manager's mouth. It was nothing but God's favor for him to have eliminated the excessive price of hiring a plumber.

"Thank you so much!" I yelled as I hugged him.

"All I require for you to do is get a certified electrician to do any additional electrical work needed."

"Yes sir, that will not be a problem."

He shook my hand again and said, "Well, it's all yours. We just have to write up the contract. We'll call you when it's done so that you can sign the lease."

I thanked both the owner and the office manager again for their generosity and diligence.

Not too long after I left the building, I received a call from Carla.

"Do you know that the owner of the salon I'm working in did not sign the lease yet? Any day the owners of the building could evict us out of there."

The timing could not have been more perfect. Carla and I both needed a place of stability to work in. The "business man" who was supposed to be taking over Steve's shop had reneged on the deal. Steve ended up closing his business a week later.

"Carla, I was just about to call you. I have some great news! I just got a building for us to open up a salon in!"

"You what?"

"They gave me an offer I couldn't refuse, and I had to make a decision right on the spot. They should be typing up the contract as we speak. The space is already built-out, and they even threw in two lines of plumbing. Can you believe that?"

"Did they really? That's unbelievable," she said.

Carla listen quietly for a moment as I told her how God laid it on my heart to go back to the business center we previously had gone to. I filled her in on all of the details of the offer they gave to me.

"You have to trust me on this one. It's really nice and I

will take you to see it."

After we ended our call, Carla immediately called her father who's a carpenter, told him about it and he agreed to help us fix it up.

On that Monday, my mother accompanied me to meet Carla at the location we were opening up our new salon in. She was relieved upon seeing it and said, "Ruby, you did really good finding this place."

It took some days before the lease was printed up, and I began to feel a little nervous about whether we were actually approved. I received a phone call that the lease was ready to sign on Wednesday. After the lease was official, I had another "aha moment."

The lease was signed and dated June 27, 2017, exactly twelve years to the date that I took a leap of faith and left everything behind in my hometown of Massachusetts, to move to Houston. God gave me a reminder that day, that He had not forgotten His promise to bring me from the wilderness into the promised land. That alone gave me an extra boost of faith to keep working, to keep persevering, and to keep moving forward. I didn't realize what seemed like the darkest hours of my life with the home invasion, was only an opportunity for God to bless me with a portion of the provision to go toward opening up the business.

I had less than a week to finish out the summer semester of my theology courses, so I had to spend that entire weekend working in order to finish it out strongly. I received A's in both of my summer courses, thus maintaining a 4.0 average.

Carla and I temporarily worked in the salon that I worked in prior to moving to Steve's establishment, until the renovations were finished in our new salon. After Carla and I finished working each day, we would go over to our salon to help her father get it ready for opening. He told us what to do, and we worked right alongside of him to get the job done faster. Carla and I were excited as we invested in different materials like paint, wood, furniture and whatever else we needed for the salon.

Carla and I collaborated using the creative minds that we have as hairstylists, to design a salon that everyone who entered would fall in love with. Carla's dad had a brilliant mind to create and execute the carpentry skills that left people standing in awe as they walked through the doors. Every challenge that we came up against that seemed as if it were going to delay progress, God somehow alerted one of our minds to find the solution. The color scheme was grey accented with black, white and a pop of valentine pink.

Carla and I tried to think of names for our new salon, but nothing seemed to fit. I really wanted the name of the salon to have a significant meaning, so I continued to pray so that God would reveal the name to either one of us.

I woke up early one morning to pick up some breakfast for my mother and son before heading out to work, and there was a car that I pulled beside with the number eleven on the license plate. God immediately dropped the name of the salon in my spirit, "Eleventh Hour Hair Lounge." I remembered back to the time when I was seeing the number eleven everywhere. However, it was only after I received the name to our hair salon, that God unveiled to me the positive reasons why I constantly saw the number eleven, a whole year before opening up the salon.

It was God's way of echoing out to me, "Although you've

been in the storm so long, and you're about to enter into an even darker phase of midnight, but I'm coming to snatch you out in the eleventh hour, right in the nick of time."

Jesus was crucified at about 33 years-old, or at the age of 11 times three. What appeared to be the worst or darkest thing that could happen to Him, turned out to be only a transition into His next dimension, which was His glorification and humanity's redemption. I didn't realize that God was preparing me to walk through the darkest hours of my life, only to transition me into the light, into the next phase of my life.

The salon was a place of rescue and relaxation for all clients who wanted to escape the stress of their everyday lives, and sit back and lounge in a beautiful and cozy, as well as peaceful environment. The pictures on the walls silently spoke positivity to all who viewed them such as: *"Always Choose Joy"* and *"Live, Dream, Believe, Love, Live"* and *"Do What's Right Not What's Easy."*

Carla and I opened the salon on July 25, 2017. All of our clients shared in our joy as they saw the favor of God on us and the Eleventh Hour Hair Lounge.

It was only a month and two days after we opened the salon, when Harvey hit landfall. Although God did not allow a drop of water to come into our new salon, I struggled to get through the work days as I went to my home without floors and walls. I was supposed to resume going to school in the fall after dropping the second-half of the Summer sessions to finish the salon. The day before I was scheduled to start my fall classes, was the same day my son and I left our flooded home to be rescued on boat from Hurricane Harvey.

I was in a state of disbelief because I thought to myself,

"Surely God wouldn't allow my house to get flooded after all of the hell I had been through within a three-month span."

I guess with my religious background, I looked for signs more frequently than I should have, and took it as a sign when God blessed me with the salon, that He was turning all of my gloom into glory, and I would get a break from mayhem happening in my life for a while. I was frustrated and confused about the direction God wanted my life to go in, but I didn't let it take me back to that dark place I was in after the home invasion.

After coming from work one day in late October, I walked through my hollowed house without walls, floors, or furniture. I walked up the stairs and into my bedroom, and laid across the bed. I came to the point of surrender and said, "Okay, Lord. What do you want me to do now, at this moment?" I'm listening." I picked up my laptop and began to write.

Eleventh Hour Chronicles

As I sat on top of the car with my son, in fear that we would be swept away by the rising flood waters, my mind drifted back to the many eleventh hour moments that I had experienced in my life. Those moments when I was in dire need of being rescued and it seemed there was no help in sight. They are called eleventh hour moments, when your back is up against a brick wall, and there is no way out but to go through the many challenging obstacles of life by plowing forward, which may seem impossible to do at the time. I wanted to ask the Lord, "Why did you wait so long to come?"

The Lord answered, "I was always there with you as my hand shielded you and carried you through life-tossed problems and circumstances."

I was the "brilliance of the light" that wiped the moisture from "your tear-filled face" so that you could see clearly. My light guided you to follow me while you were in the midst of the storm. Had I not been there to comfort and protect you in the midst of the storm, forceful and violent winds of life would have shattered and scattered your mind, like the residue of the debris in the aftermath along the seashore, or out in the roadways of its devastation. So please don't ever think for a moment that you've made it through the storm alone, without my assistance to lead you to calm and still waters. If I wasn't on the boat with you, the waves would have taken you out, but I got out of the boat and walked on top of the waves telling them to be still and behave. And just like I commanded peace to the sea, I spoke peace to your mind, snatching it back to sanity right in the nick of time. The purpose of the storm was never to diminish you or your faith, but it was to mature you and increase your faith to the point where you trust Me, when you can't feel Me or see Me near. Will you still trust Me when it seems as though your prayers are going unnoticed? When it seems as though the majority of all your prayers are answered, *NO*? Will you simply believe that I know what's best for you? If you wait on Me, the greatest that I have in store for you will soon come shining through. You wanted to ask Me, 'why did I wait so long to come?' I didn't wait, I was always there with you, guiding the pen as you walked through the new chapters of your life."

So I pondered on what God had spoken to my heart. I've come to this conclusion: One of the biggest disappointments when a person lets go of their faith prematurely, before the story of their life is fully complete, is you're here with so many blank pages, unanswered questions, and comatose possibilities. If only you continue on your faith journey, so that the author (God) could continue to write new pages of your life. He'll make every chapter better as the years go by, and the reflection of the pages become more and more like Him (the author), as we mature in our faith.

Storms will come in different forms, whether it's sexual abuse, an abusive marriage, divorce, sickness, the loss of a loved one, the loss of a job, loneliness, or what have you. Just know that God is with you in the midst of the storm.

ABOUT THE AUTHOR

Ruby Lee Sanders is a proud mother of her son, Tyquon M. Jordan, who graduated from Houston Baptist University in the Spring of 2019. She shares her various experiences as a single mother, her hardships through a tumultuous marriage, her struggles as a divorcee, and how to keep the faith through it all. It is said, "They overcame by the words of their testimony…" (Rev. 12:11). Ruby has overcome many storms in her life, and wrote this book as a testimony to encourage others to persevere through the hardships of life's storms. She is a firm believer that faith will navigate anyone through the storms of life.

Made in the USA
Columbia, SC
09 January 2020